Herbal How To Guide

Presents ...

MEETING MOTHER NATURE

HARVESTING WILD PLANTS, PREPARING YOU FOR THE ADVENTURE.

SANDY MARIE

"Meeting Mother Nature" is presented by Herbal-HowTo-Guide.com, a website designed to augment your herbal adventures with how-to information, tips, tricks, herbal crafts, and more.

This book does not certify you in any health care profession. It is a book of education only. If you decide to try something, shared in this book, you do so at your own risk. The Author (Sandy Marie), The Publisher, and all associates, are not responsible, in any way, for your use of herbs or their harvesting. Throughout this book you are told to see Health Care Specialists, and to seek Professionals, before you harvest or use ANY herb in ANY way. If you decide to skip that advice, you are taking full responsibility on your own.

You can contact Sandy Marie via:

Herbal How To Guide:
http://www.herbal-howto-guide.com
There are always fun things happening at Herbal How To Guide. As the website expands (and it will for many years) you'll find a lot of information to help you with your herbal arts.

FaceBook: http://www.facebook.com/HerbalHowToGuide
Join in on the conversations, learn from other folks who love Herbs. Click the link and 'like' the page to follow along.

DEDICATION

This book is dedicated to my Mother, Gladys G. Ericksen. Throughout my entire life she is the one person who stayed with me, who was always there when I needed someone, and who believed in me no matter what. Thank you for your love, Mama.

CONTENTS

ACKNOWLEDGMENTS

I wish to thank all my family and friends who have put up with my endless hours at the computer. Without your understanding this book would not be possible. Specifically my Mother, Gladys G. Ericksen, who has really allowed me to get this done by making sure I had uninterrupted time.

I also wish to acknowledge William R. Carpenter, my dear friend, who believed in my work and has helped me fund this entire adventure from the Website to this book creation.

Words cannot express my gratitude for CreateSpace.com and Amazon.com for making it possible to get my words into the hands of people who wish to learn this skill.

And last, but not least, my Herbal Heroes and Mentors who taught me through their great writings. To name a few; James A. Duke Ph.D., Michael Moore, Mrs. M. Grieve, and all the creators of the Peterson Field Guides, and National Audubon Society Field Guides.

Plains Pricklypear Cactus Flower
(Opuntia polyacantha)

INTRODUCTION

Do you know what plants you can eat, what plants can be used as medicine, and which ones make tools such as cloth or rope?

I'm not talking about the fatalistic scare that makes people stockpile 10,000 cans of diced tomatoes.

A few years back I was watching the aftermath of a natural disaster. The reporters were all talking about the survivors needing the basics; water, food, clothing, and shelter. To make a point a reporter featured a woman who was crying because food was running out and soon there would be no way to feed her children. In a poetic sort of ending the reporter had the camera man pan over a huge field of beautiful little blue and white flowers saying something like, "There is hope." The shot ended with a close up of the flowers.

I sat there, STUNNED! Mother Nature had provided food, for these people in need, and NONE of them knew what it was. They were starving in the shadow of abundance.

At that moment I knew I had to write this book. I had to find a way to get this information into the hands of as many people as I could. Not because of some looming disaster, but because it's basic knowledge that everyone should know.

Pictured above are the flowers from the reporter's shot. This is not the reporter's picture, but my own picture to demonstrate what I saw.

The White Flowers, Spring Beauty (Claytonia virginica) grow from an underground tuber like a little nut. It has a sweet, chestnut sort of flavor. The Blue Flowers, Violets (Viola sororia) provide a salad green and the flowers are also edible. Both of these plants often grow together in fields and lawns.

DON'T WAIT!

Don't wait until you have all the best tools, all the right clothing, or until you have your life in order. There is A LOT of information in this book, and although being prepared will make your personal adventure more successful and fun, there are only 2 things that you'll absolutely need to get started, both are books. These two books can be borrowed from your local library. In "Chapter 4: Plant Identification" I talk more about the two books you will need. However, for your convenience, I'll list them here:

1) "National Audubon Society Field Guide: Wildflowers" (get the one for your region).

2) "Peterson Field Guide: Medicinal Plants and Herbs" (get the one for your region). If you prefer to find food get the "Peterson Field Guide: Edible Wild Plants" (for your region).

Borrow the books, go outside, and sit in your own yard. Use this book to slowly help you get ready for bigger adventures.

For me, Wild Herb Harvesting (also known as Wildcrafting) has become a Spiritual Adventure; more than just a way to gather wild food or medicine. When I first started I was more of a gardener and harvester. I'd go into the woods to find wild food to bring home for my family. It didn't take long for me to realize that there was peace in the woods. The constant droning sound of traffic was gone. No phones were ringing (I turn my cell phone off now). None of my chores were nagging at me. The air was sweet with the scent of flowers. The sounds were the buzzing of insects and songs of birds. I found myself feeling thankful, and feeling the weight of the world lifted off my shoulders. This is what I mean by 'Spiritual'.

It also didn't take me long to realize that the adventure was much more pleasurable if I was prepared. What started with a paper bag and scissors for wild vegetables - turned into a small backpack with minimal but efficient supplies. Each area I went to taught me what I needed.

This book will help you prepare for and teach you how to harvest plants in the wild (Wildcraft). Through the stories and insights I will share the 'spiritual' peace of this craft as well. I've been in the field wildcrafting since around 1979. Now I honestly don't feel right unless I'm in the wild at least once a week. I used to live in the city and travel to wild areas. Now (2013) I live on a mountain, in northern New Mexico (USA), with all the wild areas as my back yard.

The picture above is of 'The Brazos', an out cropping of mountain close to my home. The word "Brazos" seems to have several meanings (depending on how it's used). It means, arms or limbs - it can also mean hug. For the people who live here I believe it has connotations of home and hug. This is the safe place, nestled under a great mountain, that protects them.

When my Father first saw the land, I now live on, he said his heart filled with such peace and joy that he almost felt like it was about to explode with love. He felt like he was 'home'. Not only are we nestled in the Brazos and surrounded by other mountains, we also have a clear view of a beautiful lake. For my Father, this land became a Spiritual experience. Actually, for all of us in the family this land has become a Spiritual experience in our own way. I hope the 'magic' of this place continues through many more generations of my family, and the families up here that I've come to know and love. However, you don't need to live in the wild in order to enjoy this craft. Even in the heart of the biggest cities you will find herbs. You just need to be ready to Meet Mother Nature and she'll start to teach you (in her own way).

I hope the information in this book will help you experience the same kind of peace where you live. Learning the basics will help you get to the enjoyable part much quicker than I did.

My goal is to get you ready for Meeting Mother Nature. I'll be helping you plan your clothing, choose your tools, prepare your body, and learn to identify herbs in the wild. I'll be sharing recipes, stories from my adventures, and tips and tricks I've learned along the way. I intend on busting a lot of the myths, and teaching you the practical reality. It doesn't matter if you are Urban or Country, there is a true abundance any place you are. True, harvesting away from pollution will result in the finest herbs. However, you'll be surprised at what is growing in your own yard.

Herbal How To Guide (http://www.herbal-howto-guide.com) is designed to augment your herbal adventures. The website will continue to grow for a very long time with ideas, tips and tricks, crafts, and further instruction. You are invited to have a look around.

About 20 years ago I realized that the herbs we need most, based on our living conditions, always grow close. Poison Ivy (that isn't displaced by human means) will usually have Jewel Weed, Chickweed, or Yarrow growing close. Fresh Jewel Weed (when you know how to use it) works wonders on neutralizing Poison Ivy. The only time this isn't true is when Poison Ivy has grown because we humans have added dirt, sod, or something to an area from another location.

When I had a fence put in around my yard (in Indiana) holes were dug, concrete was poured, and dirt was added around the concrete. Poison Ivy grew at the back of my fence where it had never been before. Jewel Weed or Chickweed did not. The Poison Ivy had been seeded from the dirt that was brought in.

A trip to Chicago really drove this point home (that herbs grow where they are needed). There, in the middle of the hustle and bustle of the big city, I found Mullein (respiratory easing), St. John's Wort (anti stress), and Yarrow (a wound herb). I can remember thinking that the herbs were trying to help, they just weren't recognized as anything more than weeds.

We (in general as a whole) have become disconnected from our world, from our food, and from natural health and healing. When you learn Wildcrafting (harvesting wild plants), you are taking a step toward re-connecting with your environment. I am very pleased that so many people are starting to reconnect.

One last thought before we get started. Throughout my years of working with herbs I've heard many people tell me that 'herbs' don't generally help them (as much as pills). When I ask these people what Herbal Professional they are seeing, and what herbs they are taking the answers are generally, "I'm not seeing an Herbal Professional." and "I bought this bottle of __(fill in the blank)__."

Do not EVER try to self diagnose or self treat a medical condition!!!

People seek professionals for their cars, for home building, for legal issues, real-estate, and many other areas of their life. Why have we decided that our health is something we gamble with? Your condition may not require a surgeon, but you can save a lot of time, pain, and money by finding other professionals in your area.

The word "Natural" does NOT mean safe!

Poison Ivy is 100% natural. Even IF something "natural" is safe, have you done an allergy test? It may not be safe for YOU. As FUN as all of this is going to be, as refreshed as all of you are going to feel, take precaution so your adventures will always be safe and enjoyable.

Disclaimer

This book does not certify you in any health care or herbal profession. It is a book of education only. If you do decide to try something, shared in this book, you do so at your own risk. The Author (Sandy Marie), The Publisher, and all associates, are not responsible, in any way, for your use of 'natural' products or herbs. Throughout this book you are told to see Health Care Specialists before you harvest or use ANY herb in ANY way. If you decide to skip that advice, you are taking full responsibility on your own.

Bloodroot Flower
(Sanguinaria canadensis)

CHAPTER 1: CLOTHING

Wild areas have taught me to be prepared. My first excursion was to get some wild garlic mustard, a very yummy green that has taken over some areas (garden escaped and evasive).

Having an active preschool son, and being in my early 20s, I was always looking for things to do with him. Like all Mothers I was hoping to enrich his life - AND tire him out just a little. A local Forest Ranger offered a nature walk for 4 - 6 year olds, in a local forest preserve. Each child had to have an adult with them, and we were all told to wear comfortable, old clothing.

The children had a delightful time learning about birds, butterflies, and snakes. The Ranger impressed everyone by starting a fire with no matches. Then, along one of the main paths at the ranger station, we were told about an escapee and fugitive; Garlic Mustard. This plant had leaped the fences of gardens all over and was now on a murdering spree, killing local plants and claiming land for itself. Each plant would produce around 500 seeds (plants in good soil could produce thousands).

We were all given a taste (after many questions were asked by this professional) of one of the leaves and given permission to come 'harvest' some that week so long as we pulled it up by the roots, took the leaves we wanted, and dropped off the pulled plants in a special composting bin. As a young Mother my first thought was, "Free food? You bet I'll be back!"

The following day I went back to those woods with a paper bag, scissors, and gardening gloves. I walked out with my harvested garlic mustard, ruined shoes, muddy pants, and covered with mosquito bites. I took this first lesson to be - wear old shoes and pants, and take mosquito repellant with me.

Garlic Mustard
(Alliaria petiolata)

That first lesson has been upgraded many times over the years. However, that's how the woods teaches you, in small steps, to make your woodland adventures more fun. While I was out there I did notice some wild onions (I learned this plant from my Grandmother) and I made a note to go back and get some of those. Yes, I stopped at the Ranger station and asked first. The guy just laughed and told me I was welcome to them, but to pick every other one, not to over harvest an area (Lesson number 2?).

That summer I learned to carry a small backpack (I think it was a Mickey Mouse one), go out early as the mosquitoes weren't as bad in that area, always have bug repellant with me, carry water and a little toilet paper, and ask lots of questions. Through the years different areas have taught me different things. I now have 'standard' clothing that becomes my Wildcrafting Uniform.

Here's How I Dress Today and Why:

* Light color (preferably white), cotton, 16 inch (or larger) square Bandana: Your Bandana has so many uses it isn't even funny. I wear mine folded into a triangle and tied behind my head at my neck (see picture below). Why this is so important:

1. If you have dark color hair this helps to keep you cooler.

2. If you perspire it keeps the sweat out of your eyes.

3. It protects your head and hair from nasty things (like tree sap and bugs). Some tree sap can be harder to get out of your hair than gum. And, face it, it's easier to pull off a bandana, when things drop on your head, then to run around like a maniac slapping at your hair.

4. Your bandana can be used as a wash cloth or towel.

5. You have a make shift bandage or tourniquet if needed.

6. Need a small clean spot on the ground? Your bandana can be spread out.

7. Put over your nose and mouth for air born problems (like pollen) and bad smells. In New Mexico we do get wind and dust.

Around the outside edge of your bandana write the words (use a permanent pen like a Sharpie), "Emergency Contact Inside". Repeat it all the way around the edge. On the inside write your name, address, name of a contact person and their phone number. This information isn't visible for all the world to read (if you have it folded over), but if something 'should' happen to you an emergency person will have it. It's always best to be prepared.

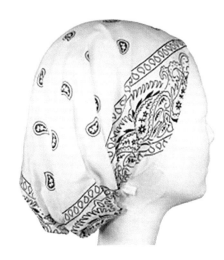

* A sun visor (or brimmed hat) to protect your eyes from the sun. You can wear sun glasses if you like, but I don't because I run the risk of missing something when my world is colored by glasses.

Here's a Picture of My Visor

No one said I had to be boring out there.

* A light weight, light color, OLD T-Shirt. I try to avoid tank tops because sunburned shoulders are no fun. However you will see me, from time to time, in a T-Shirt with the sleeves cut off or a tank top. Just be careful to avoid sunburn. Note: Do not wear sun screen, I'll talk about that one later.

* In Spring and Fall I usually have layered shirts. I start with a long sleeve shirt over my T-Shirt. As the day moves forward, the long sleeve shirt is removed.

* Stretchy pants with pockets. I try to match the color of mud in the area I'm going to be in. Don't wear shorts no matter how hot it is. If your summers get really hot get a pair of pants that are made of very light weight stretch cotton (if you sew you can make your own). You'll be walking in the woods and the bottoms of your legs will end up with uncomfortable scratches if you wear shorts. Yes, I know, everyone who's ever watched outdoor adventure on T.V. sees the people in shorts. Don't follow suit with the T.V., protect your legs. You want stretchy because you're going to be crawling around, sitting on the ground and bending over a lot. This isn't a fashion show, you need to be comfortable. Pockets are a must. By the way, my pants close at the ankle with velcro, but elastic or even tying them will

work. The point is to keep things from crawling up the inside. A hint for buying is to go into areas of a store that feature exercise clothing. Most of this will be light weight and stretchy.

* Light weight cotton ankle socks (or crew socks) to protect your ankles - for the same reason you don't wear shorts. The socks I have do not have elastic at the top, they are made for diabetics. This is a comfort thing. I don't want elastic to bind on my legs.

* ROUNDED bottom shoes, moccasins are best. The sharp edges of most shoes will actually cut into plants, as you walk, killing them. Stepping on them with a soft rounded bottom gives them the chance to spring back. I live on what we, affectionately, call Rock Mountain. The joke around here is that you move one rock to find three more (it's actually not such a joke). I knew I should be wearing moccasins but they didn't give me the protection against sharp rocks that I needed. It took me a while but I found a pair of tennis shoes that were totally rounded.

To begin with go shopping looking at the bottom of shoes. There are many kinds of tennis shoes that are rounded. Look at slippers as well, there's a lot of 'mock' leather out there. You can always use a little Scotch Guard water repellant to make them more suitable for the woods.

* Dress for YOUR body! The plants don't care what you look like. Your body WILL care how you are dressed.

I once had a student that - even after knowing all of this - felt she needed to make a fashion statement. She showed up in the group with a pretty floppy hat, a halter top, tiny little sandals, and a broomstick skirt. I spoke with her (nicely and privately) about her apparel and she (very defiantly) pointed out that I had said, "Dress for your body," saying this was what she was most comfortable in (there were several good looking young men in the group, lol). So I quickly wrote up a disclaimer and had her sign it. Needless to say, she lost her hat, was miserable with bug bites, scratches all over her legs and ankles, sunburn, and ruined her pretty skirt and sandals. The really funny end result was that the guys she was trying to attract were totally uninterested by a female (no matter how pretty) that wasn't prepared. I felt really sorry for her, but she had set herself up to learn a lesson the hard way.

* Take off all jewelry, leave it at home. I've had many people tell me that certain things they wear have great significance to them. My answer is always that - if these items mean a lot to you, leave them home so they don't get ruined. Especially necklaces, bracelets, and earrings - you could get away with a ring, but think about leaving it at home if you have any stones set into it. If you feel you need a watch, get a cheap dollar store one.

* Gloves are very important and will be covered with equipment.

You are going to be in Mother Nature's back yard. She provides some wonderful plants for you to harvest, but to get to them you'll be finding bugs, animals, mud, sticky stuff, animal poop, rocks, creeks, and all manner of outdoor wonderfulness. EXPECT the clothing you wear to get stained and possibly ruined.

Spend some time and think about what you - personally - might need. If you have a weak back will you need a back brace? If your skin is very light colored you may want to cover your arms more. Long hair might require a rubber band (or scrunchie) to keep it bound and out of your eyes. I have M.S., I have gone wildcrafting with a walker, ankle braces, and wrist braces. Whatever you need, be sure to take it. Handicaps shouldn't stop you, they may only slow you down. And, for the record, if you do have any handicaps - PLEASE - find a friend to go with you.

Dutchman's Breeches
(Dicentra cucullaria)

CHAPTER 2: YOUR BODY

This isn't about physical fitness, although being fit and healthy is helpful. I have multiple sclerosis. It doesn't stop me, it has only slowed me down. What's most important is to know your own personal limits and make your own personal choices. This isn't a race, you aren't going to be moving fast (if you do you'll miss a lot), but you are going to be walking and maybe crawling around. As the season moves on you'll notice wonderful changes in your body, they happen naturally. DON'T WAIT until you think you're 'fit enough' to go out. Heck, start in your own back yard. No matter where you live you'll be surprised at what grows wild in your own yard.

It's very important to see your Health Care Specialist before you start on this adventure. Tell them what you plan on doing and find out if you have restrictions that you should be aware of. Yes, this is a healthy adventure, however we should all be aware of our bodies before we start any new activity.

I'm totally aware of the fact that many of you will skip the above recommendation. I did, until I was about 45. My thought was that I felt good, why go to a doctor? Had I followed this advice they may have discovered my M.S. sooner. Would that have helped me? I'll never really know. Just go get a physical. Yes, it will cost a little bit, but your peace of mind is well worth it. Tell the doctor you are becoming more active and you just want a physical. That should get the doctor out of 'find something wrong' mode.

Wild Animals

Why are wild animals listed in this section? Because knowing your body is important in wild areas, and wild animals (and how you know you can or can't react) are a part of wild areas. Before you go out, do some research into the kinds of animals in your area. And, talk to local authorities about the best way to 'deal' with them should you find them. Be informed before you go out.

Note: Dogs can be more dangerous than wild animals. They are not afraid of you.

Here's what IS important:

1. Check with local authorities and learn your area. Talk to them about 'dealing' with the animals that are in your location.

2. Always be alert to your surroundings. Move slow, scan the area, look up as well as around. Are there animal tracks on the ground? Do you see animal poop and how old is it? Do you see nests (bees can be very harmful if you're too close to their domain)? The worst encounters are those that surprise both you and the animal.

3. If you start getting tired - GO HOME. You need to be alert. Many accidents happen because people have pushed themselves and they are tired. Besides, if you start associating your adventures with exhaustion you will stop enjoying them, and you'll most likely stop doing them.

4. The two worst times are Spring (many animals have babies), and the Fall (when animals are fattening up for Winter). If the thought of animals bothers you, avoid real wild areas during those times. There are plenty of parks and preserves that you can still go to.

Most of the time you can walk away before the animal gets too close. DO IT! You may want to have a cell phone ready.

If you are carrying ANY kind of food, including something yummy you may have just harvested, set it down and walk away. Most of the time you are being looked at because the animal smells the food. You can buy a new backpack and tools, you can't buy a new leg. That may sound harsh, but it is true.

Deer

Most deer will avoid you (unless you have cracked corn).

It was a warm day, late in the harvesting year toward the end of September. Some how I had neglected to harvest Mullein and I needed about a bag full of leaves and half bag full of flowers. I knew of a small stretch of wild land between two farmers. It was a nice little stretch of open field, well protected from wind and cold, with trees all around. I decided to check it out and see if there was any Mullein there.

As I entered the clearing I noticed thick green grass, stands of several kinds of wild flowers, and a lot of deer poop. Most important to me was a stand of Mullein that would fill my needs.

Sure enough, as I began to harvest the Mullein, a small herd of deer joined me. It was a wonderful feeling, being that close to the herd of ladies and just quietly working - a true Spiritual Moment! I did notice that the ladies were nervous, but instead of being alert as to why, I just figured they were nervous because I was there.

As I watched them (out of the corner of my eye) I noticed many of them suddenly laying down, and some of them walking away slightly ignoring a certain area. Upon looking at the area they were ignoring I noticed a HUGE buck with HUGE antlers. He was looking right at me and he didn't look happy. In my haste to harvest I had forgotten that it was (*) rutting season.

I thought that walking or running would have been a mistake (with M.S.). I sat down, put my head down (always keeping my eyes on him but not looking directly at him). I put my cane across my legs (to use if I had to), I slipped my cell phone out, turned it on, and set it so I could instantly dial 911.

As soon as I sat down, the buck seemed to relax a bit. He munched on some grass (always looking at me) and slowly came over. He would stop by some of the deer laying down and sniff their neck. The deer he sniffed, just sat their quietly. He worked his way to me.

Thoughts raced through my head. The power of those legs could easily overtake me in a second. The antlers were longer than my chest was wide, and as powerful as his neck and back looked he could throw me easily 20 feet or more. There was no way I was going to survive this if he got angry. I cursed myself for not remembering it was rutting season. I should have left the minute the females were herded into the area. It's amazing how religious a person can get in a moment like that. I only had one choice ... I put my head down. My heart was beating so hard that it was about ready to jump out of my chest. I could feel the heat of fear in every muscle of my body. I could smell the deep musk of this animal and ... I was crying.

He stepped over to me slowly. HE SNIFFED MY NECK! He snorted (what sounded to me like total disapproval), and walked away. Yes, as if in total disgust ... he just walked away.

You bet I gathered my tools and got the heck out of there. But what an experience! I wish I would have gotten a picture of him, but honestly he is etched deep in my memory.

* Rutting Season: Another term for mating season. This is the time of year you'll see two male deer locked, antlers to antlers, in battle for the 'right' to mate. The males only have one thing on there mind (and that may have saved me).

This is a small herd of deer that visit, where I live now.

A Little Squirrel Taught Me

Sometimes Spring, in the Great Lakes region, can be very dangerous. Especially flooding rains in Illinois. The area I lived in had many open fields (mostly belonging to farmers) so heavy rain could be very destructive. We had one such storm that included Thunder, Lightning, Hail and LOTS of Rain. As I usually did, I went to my favorite wild area to check it out. The river that ran through the area was far outside it's normal banks and running faster than I had ever seen. I was relatively new to wildcrafting, and not as careful as I should have been. I found a small area of high ground. Wanting to get a little closer, wanting to see the river, I crawled up onto this muddy rise. This small ledge had another ledge just below, followed by the raging river that was so loud I could barely hear myself think. The river had pieces of trees, homes, and other debris. It was a force of destruction like I had never seen before and I stood there shaking. I set my backpack down, took out my camera, and stepped just a little closer to take a picture.

Sink holes swallow people faster than you can imagine, I had no time to grab hold of anything. I tumbled through the hole and landed on the next ledge below. Upon landing I was sure my leg was broken. To make things worse all my supplies were on the ledge above me (about 10 feet up). To add to my pain (and panic) the mosquitoes were in feeding frenzy mode. They were thick and I was in tears trying to get them away from me.

In a strange moment of quiet I saw a Mother Squirrel, a few feet away, nursing a small brood of young. She was looking right at me. When I noticed her, she would scoop up some mud and smear it on herself and her babies. This happened a few times - I'd look at her, she'd do the mud ritual. Finally I scooped up some mud and rubbed it on my face. The mosquitoes moved away from my face. I scooped up more mud and covered my legs, my arms, my body. I later learned that mosquitoes see heat. By continuing to cover myself with cool mud I was masking my heat. This relief gave me enough time to think my way out of my situation. I was able to crawl up the ledge, and call for help. To this day I will help Squirrels whenever I can.

Bears

Mostly in the fall we have what we call Bear season where I now live. Bear season is the time that the local bears are hungry and feeding before winter sets in. It is also the time that they get very brave and not so afraid of people. If they smell food in your kitchen, they will look for a way to get in.

A friend and I were working with that morning's harvest, cleaning and hanging things to dry. This is always done on my back porch. I looked up and saw a very small bear walking right toward us. My friend did the SMART thing, he stepped inside the house. I did the STUPID thing. I picked up a piece of metal, started banging on it, and yelling at him to go away. I think he was shocked at this crazy woman he saw and he turned and headed away from us. I do remember looking to make sure he had lots of open space (and he did). I also remember realizing the STUPID thing I did when my friend stepped back outside and said, "Mountain Women just amaze me!"

The bear walked away and sat down to think about what just happened. I was able to get a picture of him, he wasn't too happy with me.

My Little Bear Friend

Back to the Chapter about your body:

Get the chemicals OFF your body! Yes, I know, this is all the rage, the current fad, the new awareness ... let me give you a few practical reasons for doing it before harvesting in the wild.

The BIGGEST practical reason is that all the chemicals and the perfumes actually DRAW bugs and animals to you. The smell of your shampoo, soap, deodorant, toothpaste, hand creams, sun lotions (as I mentioned earlier), finger nail polish, make-up, hair dye, colognes, anything that isn't natural. And this goes for your clothing as well. Laundry soap and fabric softener are a no-no (I'll tell you how to avoid these in a moment).

Another practical reason is that they will affect your sense of smell. I've tracked down herbs by simply smelling the air, and you'll be able to do this too. But you need to get all the other smells off before your nose will start enjoying the natural smells.

One of the things you'll also be able to do is animal and bird watching. I have REALLY harvested amidst a small herd of deer (see the story above). I believe they 'accepted' me because I moved slow, I kept doing my work, and I didn't smell of 'human chemicals'. I smelled fresh, natural, and part of the woods. At the end of this chapter I'll share some natural recipes with you so you can be fresh, clean, and natural.

Bugs

You will have more problems with bugs than with any wild animals. As a matter of fact, many of my students found this to be the biggest problem they faced. Even I have been forced out of areas because the bugs were just too thick. And that drier sheet in your pocket trick doesn't really help. It may get rid of a few kinds of bugs, but I've found it actually draw others (like bees and wasps).

You also need to know that natural repellents are great, but they don't last long and you need to keep putting them on in bug thick areas. So go ahead and buy them if you like, or you could even have some fun and make your own. Just be aware that they aren't going to last long.

The only solution is really to get your body ready, get the chemicals off your body, and have a good repellent for emergency. At first you may have to resort to chemical repellents. But let me tell you a secret, there are a lot of natural things you can do, to and for your body, to assist this process, so don't put the repellents on until you feel you need them. I still carry them with me (Note to myself: I should probably throw away the old stuff and buy new as I haven't used it in years).

1. The biggest advantage you can do is to become a garlic eater. The night before you go out make sure your evening meal has lots of garlic. The morning before you go out eat more garlic (garlic toast with a bowl of oatmeal, or a few eggs, in the morning is pretty darn good). But remember to use fresh garlic (not dried). Garlic will start to work in your system to repel blood needy bugs. Garlic travels through your body via your blood, and most insects don't like it.

If you know you're going into a mosquito infested area, put a small slice of fresh garlic in the bottom of your shoe, in your socks - both feet. Position it so it doesn't hurt to walk on it, but still touches your skin. You'll be surprised because within about 10 minutes (even though it's on your foot, inside your sock, inside your shoe) you'll start to taste it. TEST GARLIC BEFORE YOU USE IT. Some people do have allergic reactions to Garlic, and sensitive skin may have adverse reactions as well.

2. 24 hours before you go out, avoid ALL sugars, ALL sweet (even natural like fruit, and especially the diet sweeteners). The sweet, whether natural or artificial, actually draws bugs to you as well (and many animals smell the sweet too). Yes, the garlic will cover some of that up, but your body gives off a 'sweet' smell when there's sweet in it. Before you do this find out how a diet without sweet will affect YOU. Remember YOUR safety is in YOUR hands.

Don't expect these things to be miracle workers right away. How old are you? How much sweet have you eaten in your entire life? How much garlic have you eaten in your entire life? As you practice this the 'natural' repellents inside your body will start to build up. One day, you'll be with a friend at a park, they will be getting eaten alive and you - without doing a thing - will be bug free. That day will prove to you that it really works.

By the way - DON'T stop eating fruit! Eat lots of it on your 'off' wildcrafting days. I am not saying fruit's bad.

3. I have been told that taking vitamin B works well. I haven't tried this, but you are welcome to.

Healthy Diet

It should go without saying that a healthy diet will improve everything. So, before I get into other important things I'd like to share a few things with you concerning diet.

For health's sake, get off of all the processed and prepared foods. I am so guilty of this and I didn't even realize what was happening. I was trying to save pennies and time, I was trying to serve healthy meals, I was brainwashed by all the commercials. In other words, I was pretty much an average American, lol.

A box of whole grain oats that you can just pour milk on? It looks healthy, and wow, that's easy for breakfast.

I don't have to make my own biscuit mix?

I don't have to make my own noodles and the cheese in those little boxes is dry so it won't spoil.

Vegetable soup in a can? Grandma used to can her soup.

I don't have to make my own jams and peanut butter, I don't even have to make my own bread.

Well, I'm sure you get the idea. Then I started reading labels. There were so many things, in that food, that I couldn't even pronounce. No wonder I was gaining weight (not realizing what was happening) even though I was still very active out in the fields.

Do yourself a healthy favor, eat only one ingredient foods. That doesn't mean you can only eat one thing at a time. There's nothing wrong with doing your own mixing - just start with one ingredient foods.

If you are carrying any extra pounds you'll notice a few of them will start dropping off right away. Even if you aren't over weight you'll still notice some wonderful changes in your body. None of the changes will be over night. As a matter-of-fact, some people go years without noticing changes, then one day they wake up and remember how they were, and how much they've changed.

You also need to know your body's needs.

1. If you are on medication - bring one day's supply with you, even

if you only plan on being out for an hour. If you don't take medication but have other concerns, account for them. Even on my best days, with multiple sclerosis, I always bring my cane.

2. Bring toilet paper with you. I buy the biodegradable kind (no perfume). DON'T USE A PLANT.

3. ALWAYS bring water.

4. Always bring easy, non-perishable food. Homemade trail mix is great (but avoid sweet stuff in it). Once you learn your area you can bring a bowl and fork and make a wild salad, however, don't count on that at the beginning.

5. Bring a lighter or camping matches, something to make fire.

6. I also carry one of those silver emergency camping blankets.

ALWAYS TELL SOMEONE
YOU ARE GOING OUT,
AND WHERE YOU EXPECT TO BE
OR, GO WITH AN HERB BUDDY.

Cell Phones and Other Electronics

When I started wildcrafting cell phones and portable computers didn't exist. The longer they stay with us the more studies are being done about the effects of these electronic devises on wild life. Effects? We're not sure what the animals, plants, bugs and nature, in general, are 'hearing or feeling' with these gadgets. For me, I carry mine - but THEY ARE TURNED OFF! First, I don't want a phone call when I'm in the wild. Second, not knowing their effect I would rather not contribute to something I'm not sure of. Third, I do have them for MY safety.

As you all know I document and photograph things. My camera is with me, I turn it off until I need it.

As far as carrying the new notebooks and tablet sized gadgets, I can see the advantages, but with everything else I'll leave mine off until I need it.

Back in 2011 we had wild land fires very close to us. I stopped harvesting everything and became a gardener / caretaker of the mountain. It was obvious that the plants were suffering. All growth was stunted, blooms would appear and go to seed rapidly, leaves and stems were yellowing and droopy. At times I had to wear my bandana as a mask over my nose and mouth because the smoke was very thick.

Because I wasn't harvesting I didn't think to turn my cell phone off. Moving around was difficult, with that much smoke in the air, so I sat down on a rock to rest. Sitting quiet I could hear a slight 'humming' noise. You need to understand that we don't have traffic and other 'human' noises up here, so it's easier to pick out a noise that doesn't belong. After two or three minutes of searching my body, to find the humming noise, I found my phone. Holding it up to my ear, in this quiet, I could hear the humming clearly coming from the phone. I turned my phone off and the humming stopped. Now I'm not saying all phones do this, but it did make me realize that there is a noise. It was a pretty awakening experience for me.

Try something: Systematically go through your house and turn things off and unplug them. After you do each one, stop and make note of the increasing quiet. If you can you may want to go to your breaker box and systematically shut the breakers off. If you live close to other people, you'll hear them.

Once you have everything shut off (even if you hear others around you) sit in your quiet for a few minutes. Then slowly turn everything you normally use back on. This is just to make you aware of the noise you have gotten used to, white noise that just exists in our lives. You'll find this an interesting lesson in awareness.

FIRST AID KIT

You should carry a small, personal, first aid kit. If you carry medications with you, they can go into your kit. Make sure that the box or bag for your kit is water tight.

I am a volunteer with my local fire department. One of the advantages is that I've received training in basic First Aid by the American Heart Association. The following is their Sample of a good 'business or home' First Aid Kit.

* Absorbent compress
* Adhesive bandage
* Adhesive tape
* Antibiotic treatment
* Antiseptic swab
* Antiseptic wipe
* Antiseptic towelette
* Bandage compress (2 in.)
* Bandage compress (3 in.)
* Bandage compress (4 in.)
* Burn dressing
* Burn treatment
* CPR barrier
* Cold pack
* Eye covering, with means of attachment
* Eye / skin wash
* Gloves (make sure you're not allergic to the material they are made of)
* Roller bandage (4 in.)
* Roller bandage (2 in.)
* Sterile pad
* Triangular bandage
* Heartsaver First Aid Quick Reference Guide

There are many ways you can customize items in this kit. For example, as I mentioned earlier, this would be the place to keep your medications.

* I also keep a small bar of granola inside the kit.

* I hate wet feet so I keep a clean pair of socks in my kit.

* My kit is designed for one person so my supplies are all the smaller versions. When a 'smaller' version isn't available I break things down so I am carrying less.

* I do not carry a CPR barrier.

* I don't carry a Cold Pack as there isn't any way to keep it cold while I'm in the woods. You could bring the kind that has the chemical inside (break a small pill inside and it chills).

* I don't carry the 'Quick Reference Guide'.

* I do carry Band-Aids (a few of each size) as most of my 'wounds' are small cuts.

* I carry a tweezers, small magnifying glass, and small scissors.

* In the kit I also put my waterproof matches, a lighter, 8 oz of water, my emergency blanket, small flashlight, I carry a Leatherman tool, and a spool of jute.

* Don't forget to carry personal care items.

Even though my emergency kit is water tight, I also seal everything in individual plastic bags. I've had things leak and sweat inside and it's a good layer of protection.

If you like you can go to a natural foods and supplies shop and get more natural items. If you are going to just buy a ready made kit - OPEN IT - and see what's inside. Even with all the items mentioned above my kit is very light and compact. The kit from the American Heart Association is designed for a business (or a home with more than one person), make yours personal and smaller.

Recipes

Earlier in this section I mentioned getting rid of much of your chemical products and replacing them with more natural items. What I'm going to share with you here are the basics. I am slowly adding more and more of these kinds of recipes to the website (Herbal How To Guide: http://www.herbal-howto-guide.com), so please enjoy the free information there and remember to go back often to see what new stuff has been added.

Before I start with recipes I'd like to point out that:
1) Most grocery stores have more natural products now.
2) If you live in a nice sized city you should be able to find several shops that sell natural products.
3) Shopping on-line for 'natural' products I recommend Mountain Rose Herbs: (http://www.mountainroseherbs.com). They are not the 'cheapest' but they do have awesome quality products.

Natural Laundry Soap

You can buy all natural, eco friendly, scent free detergents. There are also many recipes online to make your own. And, if you are a soap maker you may even be able to make some homemade soap to accommodate this need. I've been researching other 'blends' for making Laundry Soap and I'll share what I find on the website (http://www.herbal-howto-guide.com) - most likely by spring of 2014. However, you can go totally natural / herbal.

First make sure you rinse all the mud off your clothing, I do this when I get home. Before you start doing ALL your laundry naturally, test with one item (hand washed) to make sure you are not allergic to the herb used.

Soap Nuts (Sapindus mukorossi)

These are all the 'thing' right now and if you hang out in natural circles I'm sure you'll hear about Soap Nuts at some point or another. If you are bound and determined to use them the best place to buy them (not the cheapest) is Mountain Rose Herbs.

I personally don't like them. To me they broke up easily, and even with the little bag I put them in I ended up with bits and pieces in my clothing. They are also an import from India. Now I have nothing against India, and I'm very happy that India has a good export. However, (AND THIS IS JUST PERSONAL) I would rather buy something closer to my home. If I lived near India - I would most likely buy soap nuts.

They also have a 'cute' name. And naming something is a big part of marketing. If they were called by their botanical name, "Mukorossi", people would shy away from them because of "Muk" in the name. See what I mean?

Yucca Root (Yucca constricta)

Right off the top can you spot why this herb isn't getting the big sales? It's because of "Yuc" in the name, lol. I'm seriously thinking of naming these, Herbal Soap Chips (or something like that).

Almost ALL dry, warm climate areas of the world have some species of Yucca. So this herb is more global and more available. Yes, I harvest this so it's good for me, but this is not the main reason I like these. I've been using this (off and on) for about 2 decades now. My Mother and Father have owned their New Mexico land for about 30 years and I would always harvest a bunch every time I came to visit. Yucca doesn't break up as easily and I don't get bits and pieces in my laundry. It seems to do a better job for me, and it definitely lasts longer (perhaps because it's a solid root).

I put 10 cut up pieces in a bag. I have three bags (with different colored string) hanging by the machine. I have a little piece of paper above the hooks so I can log how many times I've used each bag. Small load = 1 bag. Medium load = 2 bags. Large Load = 3 bags. I'm also a bit lazy. If I'm hanging my clothing outside, I hang the bag too (to dry). If weather doesn't let me hang clothes and I have to use the dryer I just throw the bag in the dryer with the clothing. Then hang it back up for next use.

Your Herbal Soap Chips (There, see how nice that name looks?) will last for several loads of laundry, but you'll need to do a little experimenting for your area and take notes. Water is different in all areas. The softer and cleaner your water, the longer they will last. I have terrible, hard, well water. We use filters to get it to drinking freshness at the sinks. However those filters are not at the washing machine. My (Yucca Root) Herbal Soap Chips only last about 7 loads. A half hour away from me, in a town, my friend's lasts about 20 loads. In the city (with chemicals added to the water) another friend can only use them for 15 loads.

In either case (Soap Nuts or Yucca Root) do not be surprised if you don't see bubbles. Bubbles, needed to get things clean, is just a myth.

Natural Fabric Softener

This one is easy. Mix a 25/75 solution of natural Glycerin (25%) and Apple Cider Vinegar (75%). Natural Glycerin, made from Olive Oil, can be purchased at many places online, and can be purchased at health food stores. If you want a smell, soak good smelling herbs in it for a week before you use it (like lavender, mint, pine, chamomile, roses, etc.) and strain the herb out before you use it.

This works BEST if it is always added to your washing machine. However, if you forget you can use it in a dryer: Keep this in a sealed container by your laundry with cut up sponges in it (cut to about 1 inch x 1 inch). Toss a slightly squeezed out sponge in as you begin your dry cycle (same as a dryer sheet).

The best way - put a 1/4 cup in the last rinse of the washing machine. And yes, the vinegar smell goes away REAL quick, so don't worry.

If you can't find Glycerin, using just Apple Cider Vinegar is wonderful. I haven't used Glycerin for a long time. Only because I'm lazy and haven't purchased any. I really don't see a difference in the softness of the clothing, but the Glycerin does seem to take care of a little bit of the static cling. The reason Vegetable Glycerin works for static cling is because of its nature to draw moisture out of the air. However, I do know some people that swear their clothing is MUCH softer when Vegetable Glycerin is used. That might be a water issue.

Deodorant

The more you get away from chemicals the less chemicals you'll need to use. This has surprised many people.

I do not use a purchased deodorant anymore, and honestly the only time I smell is if I haven't had time to clean after a real hard workout. A simple deodorant is to just pat a little baking soda under your arms. If you feel you need an antiperspirant mix 50 / 50 baking soda and corn starch and use that.

I've had a lot of people ask me for a good antibacterial to add. I use Sacred Sage (Sage Brush - not cooking sage or white sage). This is a natural antibacterial / antimicrobial. Powdered add 1 teaspoon per 1 cup of a baking soda / corn starch mix. However, Lavender is a good substitute (smells better to many people, both male and female), and is easier to get. If using Lavender use the same amount, 1 teaspoon of Lavender to 1 cup of backing soda / corn starch mix.

Native peoples, in this area, used to pack meat in Sage Brush (Sacred Sage) to preserve it and help it last longer. It really works (but does give the meat a strange taste). It is because of the antimicrobial properties that ranchers and farmers hate it. The plant actually effects the areas it grows in making it difficult for other plants to germinate or grow.

Remember; test, test, test - before you use something herbal. All herbs can cause allergic reactions in different people, especially under your arms.

Shampoo

I make Yucca Root Tea for my Shampoo. 5 cut up pieces (about a 1/4 - 1/2 inch thick) to 1 cup of water. Place your Yucca Root in the water and bring it to a boil quickly. Remove from heat, cover, and let it sit for at least 10 minutes (cool enough to touch is best, but when in a hurry I have added an ice cube or cool water). Use it carefully as its water and not a thick thing like you're used to. Rub just like you do with commercial shampoo, but don't expect bubbles (remember, bubbles are a marketing myth). Rinse well with warm water. Before you use this as Shampoo, test a small area of skin to make sure you're not allergic to Yucca Root.

Some people have told me that their hair feels dry after use. There are two reasons for this.

1) They didn't rinse well enough (it is hard to know when, as you don't have a lot of bubbles going down the drain). Rinse until your hair is 'squeaky'.

2) If your hair is dry after use you may need to use a conditioner to restore the PH balance (see below).

Conditioners, Lotions, and Creams

Just about everything else you need you can make under this category.

Herbal How To Guide: http://www.herbal-howto-guide.com. Some information is shared on the website and much more will be added as time passes. I even tell you what my favorite recipe is, and I use this for body lotion and hair conditioner, no scent added. You can also make a personal lotion, with your favorite scent, for days off. Please take the time to go to the website and learn more about this skill. You'll want to use it, with the herbs you collect, so make sure you test each ingredient before you start.

Basic Cream Recipe
* 1 part Liquid Fixed Oil
* 1 part Solid Fixed Oil
* 1 part Emulsifying Wax
* 4 - 6 parts Herb Water (or plain Water)
* Preservatives as Needed or wanted

Start by melting, over very low heat, the Cream Solids (fixed oil and emulsifying wax). Just melt it, don't let it get too hot. As soon as everything is liquid remove it from the heat and add your liquid fixed oil, stir to blend it all together. Slowly add your water while stirring. This will produce a look like Egg Drop Soup in the pan. Place your pan back on low heat and stir until it becomes creamy looking. Let this cool until you cannot see steam (if you removed the pan soon enough you may not need to let it cool). Add your preservatives and stir to blend them. If you are also adding essential oils, fragrance oils, or perfume this would be when to add them. However, I do not recommend adding fragrance or perfume to an Herbal Cream. Stir until the Cream begins to thicken. You can speed this up by placing your pan in a little ice water. After it thickens set it aside for about an hour. Then place it in your storage container.

You Can See Step-by-Step Instruction, with Pictures, here: http://www.herbal-howto-guide.com/lotion-recipes.html

Basic Lotion Recipe
  * 1 part Liquid Fixed Oil
  * 1 part Solid Fixed Oil
  * 1 part Emulsifying Wax
  * 8 - 12 parts Herb Water (or plain Water)
  * Preservatives as Needed

Start by melting, over very low heat, the Lotion Solids (fixed oil and emulsifying wax). Just melt it, don't let it get too hot. As soon as everything is liquid remove it from the heat and add your liquid fixed oil, stir to blend it all together. Slowly add your water while stirring. This will produce a look like Egg Drop Soup in the pan. Place your pan back on low heat and stir until it becomes creamy looking. Let this cool until you cannot see steam (if you removed the pan soon enough you may not need to let it cool). Add your preservatives and stir to blend them. If you are also adding essential oils, fragrance oils, or perfume this would be when to add them. However, I do not recommend adding fragrance or perfume to an Herbal Lotion. Stir until the Lotion begins to thicken. You can speed this up by placing your pan in a little ice water. After it thickens set it aside for about an hour. Then place it in your storage container.

Making Herb Water for Creams and Lotions
The night before you plan to make your cream or lotion you can make Herb Water. This becomes the water you'll use for your cream or lotion instead of regular. In a glass jar that seals place equal amounts - by volume - of herb and water (If you are using a 1/2 cup of water, you'll also use a half cup of herb). Seal the jar tightly and let it sit over night. In the morning shake the jar real hard. Then

carefully pour the contents into a tight weave strainer - RETAIN THE WATER - and press as much water out of the herb as you can. Its okay to add a little water, if you need to, to equal the amount you need for your recipe. But do try to get it as close as you can. Always remember to test an herb for allergic reactions before you use it.

One thing to remember is that using herb water will change the color of your lotion or cream, and it's not always a pretty color. Most of the time it will end up brown or green. If you really want to try and get the color of a flower petal, you'll need to make sure there's no other plant parts attached. I once tried making a lotion with rose buds. It didn't turn out to be the pretty color I wanted because of the inside of the bud. So please remember to be picky if you're trying for a specific color.

This is what a finished cream looks like.

Chicory Flower
(Cichorium intybus)

CHAPTER 3: YOUR HARVESTING TOOLS

Keeping your tools clean and in good working order is a must. There's nothing more frustrating than having a tool break when you're out to collect. I do a complete check before I start collection in the Spring. I replace any tool I need to. I clean my tools after each outing, and I do tool checks every month during harvesting season. This may sound a little excessive but years of being out in the wild have taught me to treat my tools well.

Back Pack

You need a good full sized, light weight backpack. Don't go for one of those hiking/camping ones with the frame, trust me the frame will get in the way and you don't need the extra weight. Before you buy something pick it up, find a light weight one. Look at the straps, padded straps make it much more comfortable. Think of the rest of your supplies, will they fit? Don't forget you'll be carrying herb out - is it strong enough to handle the extra weight at the end of a harvest?

Something like the following picture is just fine. What you see in the picture is my personal back pack. Yes, a little dusty, and wonderfully worn.

Hand Held Tree Pruner

This is the tool I use the most. Mine is now about 10 years old (in 2013). It finally needs a little repair. I would venture a guess that 7 out of 10 things you harvest, will be harvested by this one tool. There are two brands to look at, Craftsman or Fiskers. I happen to like Craftsman the best (pictured below) only because it fits my hand the best. Please don't try to buy a cheap one, you will be disappointed and it will be throwing your money away. If you can find a store that sells both Craftsman and Fiskers, try holding each one and see what feels best for your hand.

Good Hand Held Gardening Tool Set

The brand you pick isn't important, just make sure that they are sturdy. I've purchased cheap ones and they've bent when I try to use them. Remember that these tools are going to be used in un-plowed ground that is most likely hard and / or rocky. You want tools that are going to work for you in rough conditions. All four items, in the picture below, are needed. But you don't have to buy them as a set.

Jute

Good old fashioned, plain, ordinary jute. Do not get waxed, or craft. Just the plain stuff from the hardware store. You will often use this to tie harvest right in the field.

Paper or Canvas Grocery Bags

Paper or canvas (cloth), whatever you decide. NEVER use plastic as your harvest will be ruined by the time you get back to your car. Not because it's plastic (bad plastic), but because your fresh herb (as apposed to dry herb) will sweat and spoil in plastic.

It seems like I start every year with a good supply of canvas bags. However, in my house, people love the canvas bags and they tend to walk away. So, although I start the year correctly and eco friendly, I still have a small stash of paper bags ready when I need them.

By the way - old pillow cases work pretty good too, and for a big harvest you could use an old sheet. The point is that your 'bags' don't have to be fancy. I've sewed old towels together, and made bags from old blue jeans and other clothing items. Paper bags are really just a back up, but if you do decide to use them, get the full size ones.

Gloves

I keep three different kinds of gloves in my bag. The cloth gloves give me cushion and protection when I'm using a shovel, need to pull on something, or moving rocks. The surgical gloves allow me protection and dexterity (example: harvesting small seeds). The rubber gloves give me the water resistance and help to protect against stinging plants (like Nettles).

1. Standard cloth gardening gloves. It is important to protect your hands. Try them on to get a good, comfortable fit. Note that my

gardening gloves have thin leather, on the palm side, to protect my hand. This is a very good idea for wildcrafting. I've tried all leather and they tend to get too hot. So part cloth, part leather works well.

2. Surgical gloves, these are the tight fitting gloves that you see doctors use. Make sure they fit your hands.

3. Rubber gloves (you'll find these by cleaning supplies in most grocery stores). A good brand is Playtex but you don't have to buy top of the line. I get mine at the local dollar store.

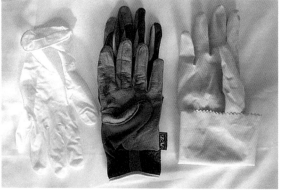

Customize

I'll give you some ideas here, your area will tell you what else you need (when you don't have it, hee-hee).

* A Scissors: A standard scissors is going to be of great use. I also carry a small one for delicate work. If you never use it for harvesting, you will use it to cut the jute. A scissors works much better on jute than your hand-held tree pruner. And a scissors is a good item to have in your First Aid Kit.

* Rain gear. Usually this can be left in the car and only take it if you think you're going to need it. When I lived closer to the Great Lakes I used to carry one of those stadium portable rain coats. I don't need it much here in New Mexico, so there is one in the car.

* Portable Chair. For a long time this was a necessity for me (with M.S.). For the last several years I haven't needed it, but boy does it feel good to sit down in the car when I'm done. I do keep a portable chair in the car.

* A staff, walking stick, or cane. At 20 I was faster than a speeding bullet, able to leap over tall buildings with a single bound ... you get the idea. Now that I'm over 50 turtles pass me on a rainy day, and rocks present a problem to get over, *giggle*. No matter your age a good walking stick comes in handy.

* Sturdy shovel. This can stay in the car for the most part, but there will be times that you'll want to use it. A small camping shovel might work better for you, especially if you'll be hiking in to the harvest area.

* A good camera that can get clear close up photos. Don't leave home without it. When I can't seem to identify something in the wild, I'll take several good pictures so I can identify it at home. There are a lot of cell phones and tablets that take awesome pictures now days. Keep that in mind to cut down on things needed.

* A pick axe. This wasn't part of my arsenal until I moved to New Mexico and Rock Mountain. Now one goes with me, but stays in the car.

* A roll of paper towel (left in the car). A few sheets can go on the walk with you.

* I have a friend that brings maps of the area they are in. Good idea! For some strange reason I don't tend to forget where I harvested what. However, now that I'm over 50 ...
With new GPS technology there might be some good ways to track your herb collecting by area. Play with different ways of tracking things until you find what works best for you. A Pen or pencil and small notebook might just be enough. And in the back of some books a log area is provided.

* A gallon of fresh water, left in the car. A smaller bottle of water should always go with you on your walk.

* Do you have special needs? Make sure to accommodate yourself.

I bet all of this sounds a bit overwhelming. Much of this is area dependent, and your area WILL tell you what you need. Review this chapter and make a list of what you think you need. Then relax and let your area speak to you. If there is something you don't use (except your first aid kit) take it out. If you find yourself wanting something, add it to your list. After a while of doing this you won't need your list anymore, you'll just 'know' what to pack.

Wild Ginger
(Asarum canadense)

CHAPTER 4: PLANT IDENTIFICATION

BE CAREFUL!
UNLESS YOU KNOW, WITHOUT A DOUBT,
THAT YOU HAVE POSITIVELY
IDENTIFIED SOMETHING,
DO NOT TOUCH, SMELL, OR HARVEST!

I had taken a friend with me to help with a Yarrow Harvest. Although she was a good gardener, and knew of a few wild herbs, she had never seen Yarrow in the wild. She studied the flowers, smelled the unique pine scent of the leaves, and marveled at the lacy look of them. She also helped me VERY MUCH that day and the harvest was a total success because of her.

About 2 days later she called me to tell me she found a field of Yarrow that was easily 10 times the size of the field we had harvested. What a marvelous harvest that would be!!! We planned to go out the following morning and she was very excited about having spotted this big beautiful field of Yarrow.

I remember she practically ran into the field and was almost dancing with joy. However, from the moment we drove up I knew it wasn't Yarrow. As I got out of the car I heard her say, "Something doesn't seem right with this Yarrow." I had to disappoint her telling her it wasn't Yarrow, but rather Queen Ann's Lace (wild carrot).

To the untrained eye there are many plants that 'could' be Yarrow. Angelica, Water-Hemlock, Cow Parsnip, Sweet Cicely, and yes Queen

Ann's Lace to name a few. This is why making SURE you have proper identification is so important. Yes, after 30+ years I don't always need my ID books, but there are STILL plants I look up.

Another little story: I was in the Great Lakes area harvesting with a gentleman friend. He was mostly there to help me with carrying a harvest out. The conversation was great and it felt very good to have someone with me. He knew just enough about this area to identify a few things. I turned my back for just a moment and when I looked at him he was eating something. He spoke, "Wild grapes." About the same moment that I looked at the plant and knew it wasn't wild grapes, he was spitting out the stuff in his mouth and yelling that they weren't wild grapes. Poison Ivy produces 'berries' that can look a little like wild grapes. Yes, he's just fine. We reacted quickly.

And another little story that asks you to STUDY! A little information can be WORSE than knowing nothing. PLEASE, study your herbs.

I had just gotten a book about wild foods. Not knowing a good book from a bad book I took all this information for absolute truth. It was truth, however it didn't tell of all the little things you should be aware of. Cattails are one of the most wonderful all year foods. Yes the young sprouts are a good pot herb, the young tufts at the top are a great vegetable, and the root makes a kind of flour much like corn starch.

A friend and I were out, in Spring, in a new wild area close to some creeks. I spotted, growing close to the water, A LOT of young Cattail. I should have asked myself why animals don't eat it. It was an easy harvest and I had a few good handfuls of this new pot herb. I was ready to bring it home and cook it up. However (and I had positive ID), I decided to taste some of this wonderful new delicacy before I brought it home. My friend did as well.

It was yummy! Within moments our mouths started going numb - followed by our throats - followed by a strange sensation in our tummies.

We were now heading to the nearest hospital (which was about an hour away). After about a half hour of terror (with slurred speech) the effects started wearing off. As we returned to normal we decided not to go to the hospital.

Did you know that the 'juice' between the leaves of Cattail was once used to numb a person's mouth before dental work? STUDY YOUR HERBS WELL! This same juice is a natural defense for the plant.

Having harvested in the Great Lakes region for decades, coming to New Mexico was a REAL treat. Oh sure, there are some plants that grow here as well as there, Yarrow, Mullein, Horsetail, Juniper, Cedar, Dandelion, etc. but they look a little different. And then, there is a whole range of NEW plants that I needed to learn.

Every time I saw something new I'd stop the car and, with book in hand, I'd run out to identify it. If I didn't have my books, I'd take a picture and bring it home.

One time I didn't have my books or my camera with me ... and there was the prettiest little purple flower. It (almost) looked like a violet when fully opened. The leaves were different than anything I had seen before, but I had also gotten used to the fact that the plants looked different here. I MADE A MISTAKE! I decided to bring the pretty little flower home and ID it there. I reached over and plucked the beautiful little thing, and POW, the pain in my fingers made me scream!

RULE NUMBER 1: Do not touch or smell until you have identified a plant. DEFINATELY don't put it in your mouth.

I broke Rule Number 1 and was treated to a painful reminder of it. What was the plant? It's called Stinging Lupine. I swear it had opened up like a violet flower.

This is a very close view of Stinging Lupine,
so you can see the little stingers.

So how do you get positive identification of a plant? There are some books that you'll find you just cannot live without, other's that

will have a few good pieces of information, and many that are about as useless as ... (You can finish this sentence, I'll get in trouble if I do.) In today's world there is also the Internet.

Let's start with field identification.

The first thing you should know is that ALL plants have flowers. Some may not look like a flower to you, but they all have them. Pine Cones are Pine Tree flowers. It is the flower that is unique to each plant.

Petal: That beautiful part of the outer flower, often in wonderful color. My youngest called this part the "landing strip," and she was pretty much correct. It is a great place for bugs to land, or board, and leads right into the center.

Many Field Guides first categorize flowers by color because it's the first thing we see. Blue (often includes shades of Purple), Brown, Green, Orange, Pink (often includes shades of Lavender), Red, White (often includes Cream), Yellow. Each book will place these in an order that makes best sense to them.

Pistil: This is usually the most prominent central feature, and the female part of the flower. It includes a Stigma (the top most section), a Style (which looks like a little stem) just below the top, an Ovary (close to the base / inside the flower - sometimes you can't see it), and an Ovule (inside the Ovary, the place were seeds are born and grow).

Stamen: These are the male parts of the flower and contain the pollen. The Stamen consists of the Anther (which holds the pollen), and the Filament (the stem looking area of this part).

Receptacle: If you look at a new flower bud you'll often see it enclosed in an almost leafy casing. As the flower opens this casing becomes the bottom of the flower (a support shelf). Some flowers look totally like the Receptacle, others lose their Receptacle after opening.

Sepal: This is a small connection between the flower and the stem.

Note: All of these parts will vary making each flower unique. When you look at some you may not be able to see a part, but trust me, it is there.

In addition to all of that, flowers are generally grouped into 1 of 5 basic shapes. Simple, Daisy or Dandelion like, Odd-shaped, Elongated Clusters, and Rounded Clusters. Yes, you will also see groupings of Fruit and sometimes Seeds.

The 2 flowers below are considered Simple. One flower per stem, symmetrical in nature, in general with 3 - 6 petals.

Left: Spiderwart / Right: Spring Beauty

The 2 flowers below are considered Daisy or Dandelion like. One flower per stem, with many strap like petals, often has a button like center.

Left: Dandelion / Right: Wild Sunflower

The 2 flowers on the next page are considered Odd-Shaped.

I have to giggle about the classification of 'odd-shaped' because it actually means that the flower couldn't be classified into one of the other sections. You might also see this listed as Bilaterally Symmetrical. Part of the description is that half of the flower 'mirrors' the other, but I've noted this is not always true.

Left: Alfalfa (the Clover Family) / Right: Honeysuckle

The 2 flowers below are considered Elongated Clusters. These are groups of separate flowers arranged on a single, central stalk or stem.
Left: Lily Of The Valley / Right: Balloon Flower

 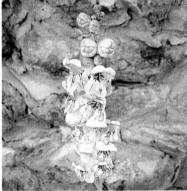

The 2 flowers on the next page are considered Rounded Clusters. Groups of flowers closely clustered atop a stem, or around one, usually so tight that the 'individual' flower is not distinguishable. Most of the Mints are in this category because the flowers are clustered around the stems.

Left: Yarrow / Right: Ground Ivy (in the Mint Family)

There are two books that should go with you at all times (read them, don't just look up the pretty pictures of flowers). Both of these can be purchased for your region in the United States. It's very important to get a field guide for your region. Herbs change from region to region and the pictures you'll see in the books will be much closer to what you are actually looking at in the wild. As I said before, all plants have flowers, so all you have to do is catch the plant when it's flowering.

For those of you who are not in the United States you can start at a Library or Book Shop and tell them you are looking for Wildflower Field Guides. From there you'll have to look at the books offered to find something that closely matches what I'm suggesting.

The first field guide (National Audubon Society) helps you get positive identification with both pictures and plant descriptions. You need to use both pictures and the descriptions for many plants. Although many flowers 'look' alike the description will help you get a positive identification. The book tells a basic description, followed by important information (like smell), followed by detail like size, how many segments, petals, etc. And finally habitat, range, and possibly comments. All of this information is important.

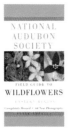 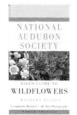 **National Audubon Society Field Guide, Wildflowers** (pick one for your region)

The second book (Peterson Field Guide for Medicinal Plants) actually tells you a brief use for the plant, but most importantly it tells you WHAT PART to harvest (root, leaf, whole plant, etc.). Plus you'll have different pictures that will give you additional help in identifying. And it tells you any basic warnings (like possible allergic reactions, or poison).

 **Peterson Field Guides, Medicinal Plants and Herbs** (pick one for your region)

You might also enjoy **"Peterson Field Guides, Edible Wild Plants"** (pick one for your region)

When you start shopping for field guides you're going to find a wonderful world of information open up to you. There are field guides for trees, edible plants, mushrooms, for all kinds of animals, and even the stars. All of the field guides are wonderful, all will be helpful, but you really only need these two.

When you come across a flower that you don't know, sit down with it. Have a good look at it and have a good look at where its growing. What is the soil like? Is it on a slope? What plants are growing around it? How much sun is it getting? Then use your Audubon Field Guide to find the flower and give it a name. Make sure to read the description, not just look at the flower. If I can't find it I'll photograph it (I seem to always take pictures, even if I do know what it is).

After you've identified what it is, look it up in the Peterson Field Guide. Does it have a use? What is that use? Ask yourself, "Is it something I WILL use?" Don't harvest "just because". ONLY harvest what you'll actually use.

So you've learned rule number 1: Do not touch or smell until you have identified a plant. DEFINITELY don't put it in your mouth.

Here's the next rule, RULE NUMBER 2: NEVER take more than 1/4 of a patch, and always harvest from the whole patch (not just one side).

You are there to thin, not to obliterate! If there's only 3 plants,

YOU don't get any! In addition, if you see a few, change your thinking into becoming a caretaker and gardener, rather than a harvester.

Our wild onions were having problems. I found some, but only 2 small clumps. I carefully divided the clumps, replanted, and moved down stream a little and planted the clumps I had separated. The following year there were 11 clumps in the area (plants like to spread by themselves too). I brought 2 wonderful onions home for that night's meal and worked again in spreading the plant. Year number 3 the little area they had started in was thick with wild onions. That was an awesome harvest! I also spread the plant to other areas on the mountain. This year the plant is back, in natural habitats, in great numbers, just like it was before, and I'm pleased that it is. I do this for all the plants. I spread seed, I save seed, I transplant, I garden. You never know when you're going to lose an area so make sure you can harvest for the rest of your life (not just that season).

And that brings me to the next rule, RULE NUMBER 3: Become a gardener, not a harvester, and you will be rewarded beyond your imagination.

Rule Number 3 brings me to another 'spiritual' sensation that you will feel. You will start to feel at home in areas. You'll start to know the areas like the back of your hand and you'll know the plants that grow there. Some of the patches of plants will feel like they become friends. You will become connected to certain areas. At first the areas will be small (maybe just your yard), but pretty soon you'll find yourself connected to entire acres and small forests. That connection will continue to grow. That connection will slowly start to change you in wonderful ways. And - don't be surprised if you start feeling possessive. I have cried over areas destroyed by both natural and human means.

When is the best time to harvest?

Every plant has it's best time of day and best time of the season. If you're a gardener you know well about 'harvesting' time. Harvesting maple syrup can only be done when the sap of Sugar Maples is running. You can't pick apples while the tree is in bloom.

Wild herbs are the same way. There are some herbs that you can harvest through most of the warmer months (Mullein leaves for example), and some that you need to wait for (Yarrow flowers).

At first, keeping a little journal of 'when' and 'where' you see something is a great tool for the following year. And, the field guides will give you an idea of when to catch plants as they flower. Pretty soon you will have it down pat and will 'just know'. Our wild onions are close to time to harvest in April. I usually start looking at them around the 10th of the month, and usually start harvesting between the 20th and 30th. After May the strength of the plant goes into producing its flower, and bulbs are no longer very good to eat.

Time of day is important as well. For the most part you need to be in place and ready to harvest as the sun is coming up (yawn). Why? Most plants rest at night (just like we do). As the sun is coming up they are fully recharged and start sending out their sweet scent (essential oils) to attract pollinators. Your goal is to catch the plants at their strongest moment. There are a few exceptions to this rule, Evening Primrose for example, that begin their cycle in the evening rather than the morning. There are also time keepers, like Chicory, that only bloom in the morning (closing up around noon - therefore giving you a good idea of what time it is). If you were to go out looking for Chicory at 2 in the afternoon, you wouldn't see any blooms.

As much as I know many of you will not like this, to be a good wildcrafter you're going to need to get up before the birds do. If you are a religious person, do your morning worship on location. You could just enjoy breakfast in the wild.

As I started doing this on a regular basis (before I learned when to harvest), I had decided to have a quiet breakfast in the woods, and enjoy the sunrise. I ate my breakfast and positioned myself to face East. Just as the sun peeked out the whole forest came alive with bird song. I was overwhelmed by the incredible experience. The following day I did the same thing in my (City) yard. I was thrilled to find out that the birds did the same thing in the City (and just as loud). I found myself wondering how many people never hear this beautiful morning song because of normal city noises and our schedules.

Mullein
(Verbascum thapsus)

CHAPTER 5:
CLEANING, DRYING, & STORAGE

I don't care how tired you are when you get back, CLEAN YOUR HARVEST right there and then! This can actually be the hardest part, not because it's difficult to do, but because you'll be tired and human nature tells us we don't want to. Yes, our backs, legs, feet, arms, etc. may be a little tired (especially at first) but cleaning your harvest is the best way to insure the best herbs. Besides, you have brought home bugs and dirt and that needs to be removed as soon as possible. (Note: Please don't harvest in areas that 'could' be sprayed with poisons and NEVER harvest close to a street where the herbs can pick up auto pollutions. Simply know your area.)

I usually start with the hose outside. Not at full force (unless I have dirty roots), but as a general cleaning. The hose also cleans me off. Rinsing them in clean water will take most of the dust, dirt and bugs off. I also do this in my 'at home' garden so I water my garden at the same time.

After the general cleaning I go put on dry clothing then go back out to get the herbs ready for drying. This will be the second look, close inspection, and cleaning.

The second inspection is done much more closely, before drying. Look under all leaves. Look closely at all stems. Look carefully inside flowers. These are all places that bugs will lay eggs and that dirt will collect. If a plant is heavily infested, put it to compost right away, get it away from your other plants and don't even bother trying to clean it. If you see a few bad areas it can just be cleaned with fresh water or that little part can be removed. Also remove any dry leaves (turning yellow) or parts of the plant that don't look good. Remember, you want the best herb possible - not the most. Quality versus quantity.

The hardest thing to clean is when you've harvested root. I have often taken a stiff scrub brush to roots to get the imbedded dirt off. With many roots the hose, on high, will get off most of the dirt, just be careful your eyes are protected from splash back.

I use one of three methods of herb drying:

1. **Hanging**: For larger plants (like Yarrow) I tie the bottom ends (always hang herbs upside down so the oils run to the ends and into flowers and / or leaves) together and hang them on my porch (it's a covered outdoor porch) out of direct sun light, on the north side of my home. I live in a dry area so this method works well for me. If you live in a humid area you're going to need to watch your herbs to make sure they don't mold. When I lived in the Great Lakes region I had a screened in porch that I hung my plants in. When the weather was very humid I had a fan that I turned on to keep the air moving.

2. **Screen Drying**: When you have small herbs, flowers, or leaves screen drying might work best for you. This is simply a frame with a screen stretched over it. Make sure the air can circulate around the herbs, and that the air flows both up and down, and move the plant material around daily to make sure things are drying evenly.

3. **Dehydrator**: A dehydrator simply moves warm air (make sure you get one with a small fan) around your plant material, in a closed compartment, to speed up drying. When I have very juicy herbs, like Chickweed, I use a dehydrator to speed up the process and reduce my spoilage.

The reason for drying your herbs is so that you can store them without spoilage. Drying only removes the water content, there is very little of the plant's essential oils and medicinal value that is lost. When your herbs snap or crumble nicely, they are ready.

Your last inspection is before you store your herbs. Obviously you want to check to make sure everything is dry. If anything bends easily or does not 'snap' or crumble, it needs to dry a little longer. However the other reason is to, again, look for bugs. There is always the possibility of missing a few during the first two inspections. At this point you can only remove and discard if you find bugs or eggs, but it's a whole lot better to find them now, than after you've put them in storage.

Storage

Storage is the biggest problem, and one that you're going to have to let your own heart lead you to.

1. **Clay pots and ceramic**: I have seen some lovely arrangements of herbs in clay and ceramic. These have the advantage of allowing the herb to breath while still sealing them away from harmful light and some moisture. However they can also draw moisture (no matter how well they've been fired), and cause spoilage (a bad pot). This method of storage is not suited for humid areas. They can also trap the herb's oils in the jar. The end result is that you must store the same herb in the same jar every time.

2. **Glass and porcelain**: I would love to have a room that looks like an old time apothecary. All those beautiful glass jars displaying the herb inside just seems like the right answer. However, these containers do not allow the herb to breath at all, and if there's any moisture left in the herb, or moisture in the container, your herb will spoil quickly. One answer is to use cork stoppers (they have the same problems as in #1). You must also make sure the jars are totally out of sun light as the glass (no matter the color) will magnify the sun's light and cause spoilage. Anything, left in sunlight, will heat up inside, so be careful with location. This is why many people switched to porcelain versus glass. My biggest complaint about this storage idea (both glass or porcelain) is the cost.

I love visiting New Orleans. There, in the French Quarter, on Chartres Street is a wonderful place called the New Orleans Pharmacy Museum. Not only will you see the way this place looked (like stepping back in history), you'll also learn about the old use of herbs and elixirs. If you get to New Orleans, make it a point to visit.

Photo from the New Orleans Pharmacy Museum
http://www.pharmacymuseum.org

3. **Food grade plastic**: With all the hubbub around plastic in today's world you really have to wonder about the containers you choose. Plastic was the best choice until I did research into the different kinds of plastic out there. There is good plastic and bad plastic, you can read more about it here:

http://www.herbal-howto-guide.com/plastic.html.

You just need to be aware of what you are buying for food storage. Those numbers on the bottom of plastic containers have a meaning. You need to look for #1, #2, #4 or #5. Never use any other number (or something that doesn't have a number) for your herbs.

4. Freezing: I've had a lot of people talk to me about freezing herbs. Again, you have to be careful the container you use. Freezing does not hurt a dry herb, but make sure you have a reliable way of marking your containers so you use the oldest first. My biggest complaint is the amount of 'freezer' space that this would take up.

Freezing fresh herbs can be a problem but well worth your effort. Every herb is going to be a little different so I suggest playing with your harvest and taking notes.

The basic method of freezing I use is simple. I start by cleaning the herb and pat it dry. I allow it to air dry for a little longer (not letting it wilt) to make sure I get a very dry surface. Then I loosely place the herb in freezer containers, mark them, and freeze them.

There are some herbs (the more juicy ones) that you may want to freeze loose first - then move to a container. To do this lay them out separately, on paper towel or cloth, and freeze, then move them to their long term container.

I've not tried freezing fresh herbs in water.

Always your best 'storage' should be to harvest only what you can use from season to season. I absolutely NEVER store or use herbs beyond one season. **This is my preference**, not a rule. My old herb goes to the compost with thanks to the herb for providing my family with food and medicine. And I always make a note of what I am composting (how much) so I can adjust my harvesting the following year.

So how do I store my herbs? I use Gladware containers, clearly marked with the harvest date. Inside the container the herb is stored in homemade cotton bags or brown paper. This protects the herb from touching the plastic and keeps sunlight out. At one time I had made several cotton bags that fit inside the containers. I am slowly doing this again. I lost all my old ones in a house fire. So, until I have my new cotton bags, the paper works wonderfully and can be composted right with the herb. Every herb has a different shelf life. Some you won't want to store longer than a year, others (like roots or seeds) can be stored for several years.

This may surprise you. Most of the herbs and spices you buy today have been in storage for well over a year, often 3 - 4 years.

Commercially, after an herb is harvested and dried, it is stored with the harvester until it sells (who knows how long). Yes, most will ship the oldest herb first, rotating their stock. These sales usually go to resellers or manufacturers who buy in bulk to reduce price. So, when you are buying, try to find a supplier that (at least) you know is also the farmer or harvester.

After the herb arrives at the reseller or manufacturer it is stored until sold or used in a product (again, who knows how long). Many herbs are stored for around a year until they are used because they too rotate their stock. If the spice has a 'seasonal' use, like Cloves and Nutmeg, this could be as long as 2 to 3 years.

If the reseller or manufacturer is also selling to a store your herbs or spices could sit in their back room until they are moved to the shelf for sale. And honestly, how long do the spices sit on the shelf? I once (as a little test) put a small dot of paper on the bottom of a bottle of Cloves (that was in the back of a shelf of 6). I had no idea how long this sat in warehouses but it was still on the shelf one year after I marked it (2 away from the front).

Now let me ask you this ... how long have your spices sat on your self? If you don't get firm about your 1 year rule (even if you bought the herb or spice) you have pretty much given up flavor and medicinal value. Until you start seeing what FRESH herbs and spices are supposed to look like, I bet you don't even realize what you are using. A customer's comment about the Yarrow I sold was simple, "Until I bought from you I thought dried Yarrow was supposed to be brownish yellow."

If you do nothing else, after reading this book, at least go through your spices and make sure you are using spices as fresh as you can get.

Periwinkle (a.k.a. Myrtle)
(Vinca minor)

CHAPTER 6: USING YOUR HERBS

SPEND THE TIME TO LEARN ABOUT EACH HERB, INDIVIDUALLY, BEFORE YOU ATTEMPT TO USE IT IN ANY WAY! SEE YOUR DOCTOR OR HEALTH CARE SPECIALIST.

1. Just because something is natural, does NOT make it safe for use, or safe for YOU to use. The word 'natural' has been over used, and used wrongly in our society and has gained the wrong meaning. Natural means that it comes from Nature - NOT that it is safe. Poison Ivy is natural, it is NOT safe.

2. NEVER try to diagnose or self treat a medical condition! Not for you, and definitely NOT for someone else. If you want to help yourself (or someone else), do the research and then bring your information to a health care specialist. If a Doctor you are going to doesn't want to help you, or tells you that herbs are no good - FIND ANOTHER DOCTOR. Trust me, there are very good Doctors out there that are interested in herbs and willing to work with you.

3. If you do use herbs, on your own, without professional guidance, you use them at YOUR own risk. You cannot sue anyone for a choice YOU make. Unless a Health Care Specialist specifically gives you a written prescription, remember it is your choice. All the books out there (including mine) are just methods of study, not

suggestions for use.

To elaborate: This book does not certify you in any health care or herbal profession. It is a book of study and enjoyment only. If you do decide to try something, shared in this book, you do so at your own risk. The Author (Sandy Marie), The Publisher, and all associates, are not responsible, in any way, for your use of herbs. Throughout this book you are told to see Health Care Specialists before you use ANY herb in ANY way. If you decide to skip that advice, you are taking full responsibility on your own.

Why am I repeating all of this? Because it's important that you understand it. Herbs are not something to mess with. Many of our powerful medications today still begin with herbs. I also know that many of you are going to just ignore those statements. Something inside you is going to say, "Yeah, yeah, she's saying all that because she has to." Actually, I'm saying all that because its the truth. If you want to get into a health care profession, go to school and learn your trade. There's much more to it then just knowing herbs.

A good Health Care Specialist will tell you 'how' to take an herb as well as 'what' to take. The problem is that these methods are no longer well known. If a Doctor tells you to take an herbal remedy as a Tisane or Ptisan, do you know what they mean or how to prepare it? If you do you are truly one of the blessed people who have learned something wonderful. This section is designed to teach you each method that a **Health Care Specialist** may suggest.

Tea
Within the last decade Tea has come to mean, "Something steeped in water." We have 'Regular' Tea, Iced Tea, special flavors (like Earl Gray), and now Herbal Tea. Tea is actually a beverage made from the Tea Bush (Camellia sinensis). When using herbs to make a 'Tea' you are actually making an Infusion or Decoction of the herb. However for simplicity, and because of today's use of the word Tea, we will start here.

Making A Cup of Tea for Flavor
Iced or Hot there are many herbs, spices, vegetables, and fruit that

just taste good as a cold or hot drink made with water, Mint for example. Making a delicate beverage with these ingredients is making something simply for the flavor. A little lemon in a glass of Ice Water is good example, it could be classified as a version of Lemon Iced Tea.

Making a cup of herbal tea for flavor is pretty easy if you just remember the number one. 1 teaspoon herb, 1 cup of water, steep for 1 minute. All of these will change a little as per your taste preferences, but remembering the number one will get you off to a good start. This works wonderfully if using a dried product, or fresh.

Start by bringing one cup of water to a boil. Remove from heat. Add your herb, spice, vegetable or fruit. Allow it to sit (steep) for a minute (you may need to strain it). Enjoy!

Making A Cup of Tea for Benefit

I'm sure many of you are aware of 'special' herbal blends designed for benefit. Go to any grocery store's tea section and you'll see blends to ease tension, soothe an upset tummy, help you sleep, etc. This is what I mean by "Tea for Benefit". I used to write down the ingredients, harvest what I could, and buy fresher herbs - then blend my own. I did that only because I know how long manufactured products 'can' sit on shelves. I think there was a difference.

This is an easy step up from the herbal tea for flavor as you just need to remember the number two. 2 teaspoons of product (herb, spice, vegetable or fruit), 1 cup of water, steep for 2 minutes - this time you need to cover the tea while it's steeping. Covering the tea will help to keep the oils in, versus them escaping via the steam. You will note that most 'tea bags' are filled with about 1 teaspoon. This is done for safety and many people will get benefit from only one teaspoon. If you don't feel you are getting benefit from one tea bag, you could try two - however, measure the amount in a tea bag before you just throw 2 of them in a cup. (Note: if you're not getting benefit, it might be the age of product and not the herbs used.)

Bring your cup of water to a boil. Remove from heat. Add your herb, spice, vegetable or fruit. Cover the cup. Allow it to sit (steep) for about 2 minutes (you may need to strain it). Enjoy!

From this point on anything you make should only include one herb, spice, vegetable or fruit. Blending should be done AFTER the creation process, unless you are otherwise directed by a Health Care Specialist. It is still unknown how some substances react with each other. You are working with chemicals, and chemicals can have strange reactions. Take the child's experiment with vinegar and baking soda for example.

Making A Cup of Tea for Medicinal Purpose - called a Tisane or Ptisan

When a Health Care Specialist suggests you take an herb, spice, vegetable or fruit for a medical purpose, as a "Tea". This is usually what they are talking about. Question them to find out if they really mean Tea (as in above) or if they mean Tisane (described here).

It's important to listen to the quantities of product that your Doctor recommends (usually 1 - 3 teaspoons per cup of water). Make sure and ask them if their recommendations are for one cup of water, or more. Bring your water to a boil, place your herb (spice, vegetable, or fruit) - loose - in the cup, pour the water over and cover it for 10 minutes - NO longer. At 10 minutes it's reached the first stage of peak potency and begins to go back down hill in a cycle (it will go back up, but not until after a long time). Remove the cover and strain the herb out of the water. It's very important to never add anything else to a Tisane for medicinal purpose - not even honey. If the medicinal tea tastes nasty (and some really do) ask your Doctor before you start adding things to it, as any addition can change the potency of the Tisane.

The cycle of cooling, when making a Tisane, brings out the first oils of an herb. These are the oils easily released and the benefit your Health Care Specialist is looking for.

Also important is to use either glass or porcelain for your boiling and your tea cup. These two substances do not leach unwanted chemicals into your tea. I have a very special pot and cup for my tea, it helps to make the experience more enjoyable.

A True Infusion or Decoction

First, the difference between an Infusion and Decoction is very slight. An Infusion is made by adding 'delicate' items (like leaves, soft vegetables or fruits, or flowers) to water, after the water is boiled. A

59

Decoction is made by adding 'stiff' items (like seeds, roots, or stiff vegetables or fruits, often peels) during the water boiling process, and covering the container while it's boiling.

To tell if you should use the Infusion or Decoction method there is a simple test. Squeeze part of your product between your index finger and thumb. If it changes shape, breaks easily, or bruises you need to use the Infusion method. If it doesn't change (like a seed or nut doesn't break) then you need to use the Decoction method. Some things are just choice. I prefer to use the Decoction method with things like Celery and Citrus peels, even though the little test tells me I can bruise them.

In both cases you will need to add as much water as it takes to completely cover the product. I use canning jars to make this so I test the amount of herb, spice, vegetable, or fruit - to the amount of water I need before I start the process.

Infusion:

Fill your jar with what you're infusing (the herb, spice, vegetable, or fruit). Then add water until the water covers the product. Pour the water into a pan, using a strainer. The herb goes back into the jar. Bring the water to a boil and pour it over the herb in the jar. Cover with a loose cover to start with (I just use any top that will fit over without sealing it - like the inside section of the canning lid, without the outside screwed on). Walk away from your concoction until it's cooled (about an hour or two). Then seal it up and shake vigorously for about 2 minutes. Total time to leave it sealed is 8 to 10 hours.

Strain the herb out and store this in your refrigerator. It should only be refrigerated for two days after it's made. So only make enough for two days use. Take as directed by your Health Care Specialist.

Decoction:

Again add the product first, and pour water in until it's covered. Dump both water and product into your pan (or just do this in the pan). Bring the water to a boil and then transfer the water and product back into the jar. Cover with a loose cover to start with (I just use any top that will fit over without sealing it - like the inside section of the canning lid, without the outside screwed on). Walk away until it's cooled (about an hour or two). Then seal it up and shake vigorously for about 3 - 4 minutes. The harder the herb, the longer you'd shake. Total time to leave it sealed is 8 to 10 hours.

Strain the herb out and store this in your refrigerator. It should only be refrigerated for two days after it's made. So only make enough for two days use. Take as directed by your Health Care Specialist.

Both Infusions or Decoctions should be made in glass or porcelain. Keep out of direct light during the steeping process. I make these at night, before I go to bed, and they are ready in the morning.

For the below items anything you make should only include one herb, spice, vegetable or fruit. Blending should be done AFTER the creation process, unless you are otherwise directed by a Health Care Specialist.

Tinctures (also called Extracts or Elixirs)

A Tincture is an herb, spice, fruit, or vegetable, mixed with a strong, liquid, edible substance, and allowed to 'steep' for 3 months before removed, strained, and bottled for use. Your herb, spice, fruit, or vegetable is added to a canning jar. Your strong, liquid, edible substance is added until it covers the product. Please remember that these are VERY strong substances and should ONLY be used as directed by a Health Care Specialist.

Honey:

Don't ever give a Honey Tincture to a child under 3 years old. If a Health Care Specialist accidently prescribes it, STOP and question them!

If you are making a Honey Tincture, keep in mind that the sugar content inside is going to want to ferment (the pressure of fermenting items can explode). No one told me this when I started and I ended up with Honey Tincture on my ceiling. One easy way to avoid this is to unseal the jar once a day. This allows the pressure to escape. Even with doing this, be careful. I once had a Honey Tincture lid hit the ceiling, and I had just opened it the day before.

Don't let this frighten you - just be careful.

Honey Tinctures should be made in very small amounts. Use no more than a half cup of honey at time. Aside of wanting to expand and ferment, honey also wants to crystallize making it difficult to use.

Maple Syrup:

First be very careful to make sure you have PURE real Maple Syrup. I don't even buy mine from a grocery store anymore because I just can't trust how it's made. I go straight to the farms that are making it (and only when I trust the folks).

Like Honey, because of the sugar content, Maple Syrup will want to ferment or crystallize so work with small amounts, only a half a cup at a time, and be careful. Also, like working with Honey, the easy way to avoid fermenting is to unseal the jar once a day. This allows the pressure to escape. Don't let this frighten you - just be careful.

To Prepare Honey or Maple Syrup Tinctures

Place about a half cup of herb, spice, vegetable, or fruit into a glass jar. Don't use a powered product, but do make sure it's cut or chopped small. I strongly recommend using dried product to reduce the film and gunk that can collect when using fresh.

If your honey or maple syrup is very thick you can warm it. NEVER place it in a microwave oven to warm. Warm slowly, over very low heat, in a small sauce pan. If you don't want to remove the product from it's bottle, place it in hot water to warm it. DON'T let it boil or even bubble. Just warm it.

Carefully and slowly pour your honey or maple syrup over the product in the jar. I suggest you pour some, then wait a bit to let it settle. Make sure all produce is covered with about a 1/4 inch more in the jar.

If possible don't seal this, just use a good cover or cork stopper. But, have a 'seal' handy to shake it with. Store this in a cool dark place for 3 months. Check it every day. If it's sealed remove the seal to release pressure. Every day you want to shake this hard (to bruise the herbs).

After the 3 months you want to strain the solid product out (discard this). I suggest warming it a bit, again don't let it boil or bubble. Pour through a fine strainer, then move it to its final bottle.

Both Honey or Maple Syrup Tinctures will last about 3 - 6 months (depending on your climate, the freshness of the honey or maple syrup, and the herb you use) after they are made.

Hint: When making a honey or maple syrup tincture you could use a corked bottle instead of a sealed bottle. If it does ferment, it will only blow its cork (and now you know one place the phrase, "don't blow your cork" came from).

Fresh or Dried Product?

Many times I'm asked, "Which is better to use, fresh or dried product?" There are advantages and disadvantages to both, so it becomes a personal preference. You will hear very opinionated options for both dried or fresh produce. Go with YOUR heart!

1. **Ratio**: There are times you may find a recipe you want to try. If your recipe calls for fresh product and all you have is dried, double the amount called for. If your recipe calls for dried product and you want to use fresh, half the amount called for. Fresh herb is always bulkier than dried. There are some books that say the ratio is times 3, some that say the ratio is times 2. In my years I've found times 2 to work best.

2. **Fresh produce** will add a water product to your tincture. This often also appears like a gunk in the jar. When it's time to strain you'll need to remove this first (if it's on the top) or pour carefully (if it's on the bottom.

I have found that fresh produce tinctures don't seem to last as long as dried produce tinctures. Perhaps it's the water content added.

There are many people who say that fresh produce adds water soluble vitamins and minerals that dried does not.

3. **Dried produce** will often absorb some of liquid you add. It's okay to 'top it off' as this happens.

I have found that dried produce tinctures seem to last a month or two longer than fresh.

Dried produce tinctures seem to be (this is by taste, not tested) a little stronger.

White or Apple Cider Vinegar:

Vinegars taste nasty to me (this is personal, many people love them). However, if alcohol is a problem for the person that's been prescribed the Tincture, Vinegar is the best alternative. Keep in mind that a Vinegar Tincture will only remain potent for 1 - 4 months after it's strained and bottled for use. After that the potency will begin to decrease at a rather rapid rate. This potency decrease will depend on the herb and vinegar you use, so it's impossible to tell you just how long it will last after the first month. Also note, a vinegar tincture needs to sit for the first 3 months, unopened, like other tinctures. The 1 - 4 months of potency begins after it's opened.

Add your herb (spice, vegetable or fruit) to a canning jar. Pour in vinegar until it just covers the herb. Seal this and shake it. Note the date on the jar. Every time you pass your tincture shake it up again. After three months time pour the mixture out through a good cloth to catch the herb. Squeeze the cloth real good to get all the liquid out. The herb is discarded. The liquid is bottled for use.

Note: If you wish you could allow the Tincture to sit in the original jar for a few days. There will be some settling (sometimes floating). By allowing it to sit you can avoid having the settlings in your use containers. I use a turkey baster to remove only the part of the tincture I want. This holds true for all the rest of the tinctures below as well.

Wine:

When my Doctor would prescribe a Tincture for one of my children I would ask if I could use Wine to make the Tincture (as apposed to vinegar). About 90% of the time the Doctor would tell me it was okay. There were certain Tinctures that aided 'MY' children on a regular basis. These I would keep 'cooking' for use. If it was something someone needed right away, I would resort to Infusion or Decoction.

A Wine Tincture remains potent for about 1 - 3 months after it's strained and bottled for use. It can also be refrigerated to extend the potency for an additional month.

Add your herb (spice, vegetable or fruit) to a canning jar. Pour in wine until it just covers the herb. Seal this and shake it. Note the date on the jar. Every time you pass your tincture shake it up again. After three months time pour the mixture out through a good cloth to catch the herb. Squeeze the cloth real good to get all the liquid out. The herb is discarded. The liquid is bottled for use.

Do some study before you start. What exactly is your wine made of and how will the herb and wine react when used together?

Vodka (or Everclear):

Trust me, 80 proof is JUST FINE. You don't need to 'over kill' by buying 100 proof Vodka or Everclear. However, they are included here for the RARE case that a Doctor would call for it. What kind of case is a RARE case? Usually someone who is dying.

Making Tinctures with Vodka is the most standard way of making them. They stay potent for about a year (depending on the herb used) after they are strained and bottled for use. Vodka is also the only liquor that (for the most part) doesn't change the properties of the herb inside. In addition they can be mixed with other things to create an end product (like mixed with honey), or blended together easily with other Vodka Tinctures.

If used in cooking (like making your own extracts), the alcohol will cook away, leaving the flavor. Take for example Vanilla Extract - yes you can make your own using this method, but vanilla beans are VERY expensive. I can now see all the bakers out there smiling because they just learned how to make their own Extracts.

Add your herb (spice, vegetable or fruit) to a canning jar. Pour in the Vodka until it just covers the herb. Seal this and shake it. Note the date on the jar. Every time you pass your tincture shake it up again. After three months time pour the mixture out through a good cloth to catch the herb. Squeeze the cloth real good to get all the liquid out. The herb is discarded. The liquid is bottled for use.

Baking Extracts:

For all of you bakers out there here is a method for making your own extracts. Only use 80 proof vodka, and make sure it's a good brand without additives. Using fresh material (as apposed to dried) is best, however good, fresh dried herb can also be used. Small jelly or jam jars, with a good sealing lid, is a good size. You want to make a cup or less at a time. Cut your herb, spice, vegetable or fruit into pieces about 1/4 inch. Fill your chosen jar to about a 1/2 inch from the top (don't pack it in, just fill it). Add your vodka slowly and make sure it settles just above the solid material in the jar. Seal the jar and shake it very vigorously for about 2 - 3 minutes. Label your jar with material and date, and set it in a dark place for about 1 month. Shake it every few days while it's 'cooking'. After the month strain the solid material out, use a piece of cloth and squeeze the cloth real good to get all the liquid out. Discard that herb. Repeat this process 2 more times. The reason you repeat is that the flavor must stand up to baking temperature. If you need to 'top off' the vodka between pressings go ahead.

At the end (after your last squeeze) you'll leave the liquid sit in the jar for a day or two so all the 'after material' settles. A turkey baster works well to get the clear liquid out, leaving the settlings (to be discarded). Your extracts are strong and will be a delight to bake with. Note that your creations may be much stronger then what you buy in a store (this depends on the herb, spice, vegetable or fruit you use). Experiment with your extracts and note (right on the jar) what works best for you. I personally find using about half the amount, as called for in most recipes, works best.

Also keep in mind that your extracts will vary from creation to creation. This variance is due to the normal and natural changes in the solid material you use. You are not using additives (like most manufacturers do) to stabilize strength and taste. I will wager that once you make your own (and find out how superior they are) you will not want to ever buy a manufactured extract again.

Brandy (or other Liquors):

This includes Gin because the flavor of Gin, as with Brandy and other Liquors, is created by the specific use of other plants and chemical flavorings. All Tinctures made with this can have a reaction with the herb, spice, vegetable, or fruit you are going to use. Personally, I don't buy or make Brandy Tinctures for that very reason. I feel that people who are touting Brandy Tinctures are really telling me they just know how to make a darn good Tincture and haven't really studied the herbs used, or the reaction they have with the liquor. I know - maybe they have, and I shouldn't be so harsh - but in my several decades of working with plants I've found more people that don't know, than those that do.

Add your herb (spice, vegetable or fruit) to a canning jar. Pour in the Liquor until it just covers the herb. Seal this and shake it. Note the date on the jar. Every time you pass your tincture shake it up again. After three months time pour the mixture out through a good cloth to catch the herb. Squeeze the cloth real good to get all the liquid out. The herb is discarded. The liquid is bottled for use.

This is also how Cordials are made, although they are often re-steeped with fresh herbs (spices, vegetables, or fruit) once a month for 2 months versus 3. Cordials scare the bejeebers out of me because they are usually made by people, untrained in the use of plants, and are blending for flavor. On top of that Cordial makers are 'cooks' who tend to keep their 'exact' recipe a secret. A Cordial could raise a person's blood pressure (especially someone who already has this problem) to dangerous levels if made with Cinnamon or Cloves. If the 'secret' ingredient happens to be Grapefruit, it could dangerously affect someone on heart medication.

**Do everyone a big favor
by completely sharing
all ingredients on
EVERYTHING you make.**

Solvent Extracted Essential Oil

No book, on the use of herbs, is complete without sharing how to do this. Before I learned this method I actually set up a still in my basement. What a terrible mess and costly experiment that was. During a distilling time a mouse crawled into the heating element (it was cold outside) and the entire still blew up. That was a mess I never want to experience again. However, my basement smelled wonderful for months after.

For this you WILL need 100 proof Vodka or Everclear. You need the higher alcohol volume to make this work.

You will also get far better results by using fresh herb, spice, vegetable or fruit (as apposed to dried herb). And, guess what, as a Wildcrafter getting the fresh stuff has just become easy!

Step 1: Follow the directions for making a Vodka tincture, above. That part doesn't change except using fresh product.

Step 2: Strain the herb and Vodka after the 3 months. Do not squeeze this. I let it drip for a few hours to get as much out as I can. If you squeeze fresh product you'll be adding a lot of gunk (for lack of a better word) to your mixture. Throw the herb away.

Step 3: Place the jar of Vodka in the freezer for about 4 hours (each herb will be a little different, so watch it and take notes). There are three substances in this. You have the water from the herb, the alcohol from the vodka, and the essential oils from the plant. Each freezes at different rates. All of these substances will separate in the freezer. Note: if you use a clear glass container in the freezer you'll be able to watch it better.

* The Vodka will not freeze in the amount of time (if at all). Alcohol has a very high freezing point and most home freezers do not reach that point.

* Water freezes very fast and will form ice crystals (maybe even a layer) in the vodka.

* Oils have a slightly higher freeze rate than water (some won't freeze).

Step 4: With a little work, and often a glass eye dropper, you'll be able to siphon off the Essential Oil and scrape out the frozen water.

Save and clearly mark the Vodka for use, WITH THE SAME HERB, again.

Depending on the plant you use, and when you harvested it, you may get a decent amount or just a few drops. Remember that harvesting, first thing in the morning, is when the herb is most potent with its essential oils. This isn't a method to use for becoming a manufacturer. But for home use, via repeated processing, you will enjoy some wonderful Essential Oils. Have you ever priced Rose Essential Oil? The price is outrageous. It takes pounds and pounds of roses to produce Essential Oils for sale. However, for personal use (especially soap making), the cost is GREATLY reduced by making your own. And, there are some Essential Oils that just are not available. Lilac for example (one of my favorite smells) is not available, as an Essential Oil, as the plant has very little medicinal or aromatherapy value. I just happen to love the smell and so I make my own.

Cooking

Cooking with wild plants is a whole new, wonderful experience in the Culinary Arts. As a matter of fact there are wonderful books that focus totally on edible wild plants. And, I'm pleased that many of the books ALSO say to only introduce ONE new food at a time. Go to your local library and I bet you'll find a lot of new recipes, using wild plants, to bring into your home. Local libraries often feature local books on plants.

There is also a Peterson Field Guide that will help you identify wild edible plants in your area, plus it tells you what part to harvest. This book was a blessing to me, as a young Mother, as I could pretty much eat my yard when finances got a little short.

I'd like to share two recipes using Dandelions. However, before I do here's a little story: After I learned the two recipes below I found I loved cooking up my Dandelions and eating them. What I didn't realize is that when you 'use' Dandelions, they tend to go away. So while my neighbors had beautiful yards filled with bright yellow sunshine flowers, just begging to be eaten, my lawn was barren and a solid, drab, deep green (hee, hee). I did start asking neighbors if I could harvest their Dandelions (making sure they never poisoned them). And strangely enough, after sharing the recipes, their lawns went barren too.

Moral of this story - DON'T harvest all your Dandelions, let some go to seed so you have a good crop the following year.

Dandelion Flower Fritters

Remember to check for allergies before feeding this to anyone.
Ingredients:
Beautiful, newly opened, Dandelion Flowers
Unflavored Natural Yogurt
Cornmeal or Ground Oatmeal
If deep frying or pan frying, use Olive Oil

Harvest your flowers and wash them right away. You don't want little bugs in your fritters. You'll need to cook these as soon as possible, after harvesting, as they will begin to close right away. Cut off the stems, leaving about a quarter inch so they can be grabbed and eaten. I've gotten to the point that I harvest them this way.

Place a few tablespoons of Yogurt into a small bowl, and your cornmeal (or ground oatmeal) into another bowl. Picking the flowers up by the stem (flower side down), dip them lightly in the yogurt, and coat them with the cornmeal (or oatmeal).

There are a few fun ways to cook these:
1) You can deep-fry them. Drop them, a few at a time, into your deep fryer and cook until the coating is a nice golden brown color.

2) Pan fry them by placing a few tablespoons of Olive Oil in the bottom of a fry pan, place your fritters - flower side down to start - and cook them until golden brown. I keep them moving like a person would using a wok.

3) Bake them on a cookie sheet, flower side down, at 350 for 20 - 25 minutes. Check them often when baking as you may need to take them out sooner or bake a little longer (depending on the size of the flowers). This worked great when I lived at sea level. Now that I live in the mountains (at 7,800 feet above sea level) mine cook for about 5 minutes longer.

Varieties: If you have a favorite coating method (like for mushrooms or onion rings) use your coating method. Spice your cornmeal or oatmeal with basil, garlic power, and onion power for a new flavor. Get creative with your spices. When I'm serving a Mexican meal, I season the cornmeal with Chili Powder. When I'm serving these with Potato Soup I simply season with Pepper or add a little Parmesan Cheese. You can also dip your flower heads into pancake batter and fry them up like you would pancakes (only they won't be flat).

Dandelion Leaf, Tomato Pesto

Remember to check for allergies before feeding this to anyone.
Ingredients:

1 1/2 cups fresh Dandelion leaves, cut about 1/2 inch wide, and packed

1/2 cup fresh Tomatoes, crushed or minced (drain extra liquid)

1/4 cup grated, fresh Parmesan cheese

1/3 cup Olive oil

3 tablespoons Pine Nuts or Walnuts (peanuts are also yummy)

3 Garlic cloves, finely minced

Place Dandelion leaves and Tomatoes, in small batches, in a food processor or blender and whip until well chopped (do about 3/4 cup at a time). Add about 1/3 of the nuts and garlic, blend again. Add about 1/3 of the Parmesan cheese; blend while slowly adding about 1/3 of the olive oil, stopping to scrape down sides of container. Process the Pesto until it forms a thick smooth paste. Repeat until all ingredients are used, mix all batches together well. Serve over pasta. Pesto keeps in a refrigerator about one week, or freeze for a few weeks.

Oil Note: Many people prefer NOT to use all the oil, and will stop adding oil when moist. This is just fine.

Dandelion Leaf has a bitter taste, unlike making Pesto with Basil. My family loves the flavor, however I've also heard this made with 1 teaspoon of honey to 'sweeten' it up a little. My suggestion is to try it the way it's described here first. Then PLAY with the recipe until you get it the way YOU love it.

Try this with other edible herbs too. What delightful flavors can you come up with?

Crafts

As you start studying herbs, individually, you will run across some wonderful stories about their historical use. These are the stories I love. For example; The tall stalks of Mullein are also called Aaron's Rod as this is the fabled stalk he used as a walking stick. Old stories of using Lizard's Tail in a potion was referring to the plant, Saururus cernuus L., not the tails of poor little lizards. The history of plants is a very rich and beautiful one, and I know you're going to love all of your discoveries.

There are many, many wild herbs that also have 'Crafts' associated with them. Broom Weed was used to make brooms. Pine Cones make great bird feeders. Make your own walking stick using a Mullein stalk. Yarrow sticks are the traditional sticks used in the I-Ching. Many plants produce fiber to make cloth, Yucca and Cattails to name two that aren't well known. Every area has plants used to make dyes, and you will always find a plant that makes a kind of soap.

So many things are, and can be, made from plants, that the list would create several books all by themselves. Before we became so industrialized, people knew what local plants to use to make the things they needed. This knowledge has faded as we rely more heavily on having things made for us. It is my hope that each of you will take up the adventure of learning about your own areas, and what to do with the plants you have.

Dandelion Root Blessing Beads:

A Story from The 1700s, Europe: In a little shire several kilometers from London (it is said) that a Priest told a woman who was barren to go dig Dandelions, make them into beads, and bring them back for his blessing. He would bless the beads, she should wear them with great faith, and when they broke a child would come into her life.

By the time the woman returned the Priest had already moved on to the next village (Was he just trying to get rid of her?) and she would not see him again for a year. She prayed, with the beads in her hands (Could this be the first prayer beads?), great faith in her heart, and put the beads on around her neck. Each night she prayed with the beads seeing herself with a small child.

Three months later one of the beads broke. The following day the woman's village was attacked by barbarians and many people were killed in the battle. This left many children without parents. The woman took ALL the children in with great joy in her heart. Even with the loss of so many lives, her prayer to have children had been answered.

Of coarse this is just a story. It's the kind of fun stories you'll find when you study herbs.

How to Make Dandelion Root Beads:

Have you ever dug up Dandelion Roots? If you look closely you'll see they have a white center. Dig up your roots (get as much of the root as you can). Wash them very well (I use a scrub brush). Cut them to the length size you want. Using a small nail or pin (depending on the thickness) push out the white center. The centers do come out very easily. Allow them to dry (I hang them on a string). Yes, if you use them, as they are, they will eventually break. But they do make wonderful beads to play with.

I have experimented with lacquers and other coatings. I have to tell you, coating the beads greatly extends their life, but I've not found an 'easy' way to do it. Currently I dip the beads, while on a thick string, and allow the coating to dry. This also requires moving the beads on the string often so they don't 'stick' to the string. The beads turn out to be a wonderful, earthy, wood - and very unique bead.

So why have I picked on Dandelions? Almost everyone can find Dandelions around their homes. It is one of the most widely spread herbs around the globe. The leaves have been used in salads for centuries and I'm sure some of you have also heard of Dandelion Wine.

Over the last 50 years or so they have lost popularity as a food because of their bitter taste (we have become a sweet loving people). So here's a secret to get the 'bitter' out. First thing in spring go out and cover your Dandelion leaves with something. It's their deep green color, created by the reaction of the sun hitting the leaves, that causes the leaves to be so bitter. If the leaves are protected from the sun, they will have a much more 'palatable' taste. I personally have grown to love the bitter flavor, but it might surprise you at first.

CHAPTER 7: 10 MOST COMMON HERBS
(Often found in your own yard.)

This is by NO stretch of the imagination a full and comprehensive list of herbs that you could find in your yard. The section is simply designed to get you outside, and get you started on your adventure. The herbs I've listed here are the ten most common useful weeds / herbs found in most yards. Trust me you will find many others in your own yard, but these will help you get started.

There are only three reasons why your yard may not have herbs. If you don't have any plants growing in your yard (and you don't know why) you may want to have the area checked for poisoning.

1) Your yard has been chemically treated to kill everything except grass, or someone (even animals can do this) has been an obsessive weed killer.

2) You've just had new sod laid or you don't have any dirt (there are some kinds of silt and sand that may be barren).

3) Your yard has somehow been poisoned by other means than the purpose of getting rid of weeds. This can include things like automotive fluids, recent building with chemical spills (includes places being sprayed, prior to building, to kill plants), fire or flooding, invasive plant takeover.

There's a 95% chance that you will see, at least, one of these most common 'yard herbs' on your property. I have 5 of them in my own yard, and my yard is mostly rock.

Chickweed, Mouse-ear (*Cerastium fontanum*)

2 other varieties (not included): Chickweed; Starwort (Stellaria media), and Chickweed; Star (Stellaria pubera).

General Description: This low growing perennial spreads horizontally taking over areas in patches. Mouse-ear Chickweed is known for small fuzzy leaves (that look like little mouse ears), slender stems, and it's tiny little white flowers.

Flowers: Get a magnifying glass if you want to see the detail of these 1/4 inch (6 mm) wide flowers. They are considered 'Simple' with 5, deeply notched (making it almost look like 10) petals. Depending on your area they will start flowering around February or March, all the way through September or October.

Leaves and Stems: The tiny leaves (about 1/2 inch (1.5 cm) are paired (making it look even more like little mouse ears) along the main stem, with no 'actual' stem of their own. Between each pair of leaves, on the stem, you'll see one line of little hairs.

Fruit or Seed Pod: Also small, cylindrical (almost looking like little horns), and carrying many, many little seeds slightly larger than the size of a pin head. In other words, they look like dirt particles.

Habitat and Range: Chickweed loves disturbed soil (like your garden) and will find it's way to just about everyone's home. Gardeners, who don't know the uses, will consider it one of the more troublesome weeds to get rid of. It is a naturalized herb that first came from Europe.

Parts To Harvest: All the books say, "leaves." But honestly I'm not going to sit there pulling off those tiny little mouse ears. I grab Chickweed by the handful. Shake it real good to spread the seed, and fill up a bag.

Note 1: In the fall mark your Chickweed patches with a long stick. This is one of the plants called a 'winter green'. No, they are not technically 'ever-green' (nor do they taste minty) but they do retain their color under the snow. When you are craving something fresh, go dig some up. Just be careful not to take the whole patch as winter is the only time this plant can actually be stopped / killed by harvesting.

Note 2: If you ever run into an old 'witches' recipe for a potion or spell that calls for 'mouse ears' this is the plant that the recipe is referring to. NOT the ears off poor little mice.

Note 3: It got the name "Chickweed" because chickens (and other birds) LOVE it. It's a wonderful, fresh treat for any kind of bird.

General Uses: Chickweed has many folk claims from curing obesity, to healing skin irritations, constipation, and coughs and colds. Let me set a few things straight. Chickweed is a salad herb that also makes a wonderful pesto, and is great in smoothies. It does not have any powerful healing chemicals more so than other vegetables. It contains vitamins A, B complex, C, D, iron, calcium, potassium, phosphorus, zinc, manganese, sodium, copper, and silica. Enjoy it as the healthy salad herb it is.

Warnings: The biggest two warnings I give you are;

1) Test to make sure you are not allergic before you take a big mouthful.

2) There are other poisonous plants that grow the same way Chickweed does. For example; Spotted Spurge (Euphorbia maculata) also grows close to the ground and has paired leaves. CHECK the flowers as they are different and check the sap which is white and milky looking in Spotted Spurge. Chickweed's sap is clear - green, and juicy. Another non-edible plant that grows close to the same is Doorweed or Oval-leaf Knotweed (Polygonum arenastrum). Its slender stem has alternate leaves, and again the flowers are different.

Remember Rule #1: Make sure you have positive I.D.

Chicory (*Cichorium intybus*)

General Description: In the wild Chicory isn't one of the most beautiful plants. It has a ragged, stiff stem with many stalkless flowers. If anything actually 'looked' like a weed, it would be Chicory. Over all height ranges from 12 to 52 inches (30 - 130 cm).

Flowers: The flowers are very showy and range from deep blue, through pink and even sometimes white. They are considered Daisy / Dandelion like with heads about 1 1/2 inches (4 cm) wide, and have sharply pointed petals, fused to the center, with several dark blue anthers. The plant flowers from last frost to first frost, approximately May or June - September or October.

Note 1: The flowers are one of nature's time tellers. You will only see them in the morning. So if you spot a Chicory plant that has several closed flowers, you know it's after noon time.

Leaves and Stems: The large leaves at the base can be mis-identified as dandelion and are about 3 to 6 inches long (7.5 - 15 cm). As you look up the stem they become much smaller, oblong and grab around the stem tightly.

Fruit or Seed: This is hard to distinguish from simply being a dead flower.

Habitat and Range: I call Chicory an American Roadside Attraction because the best place to find it is along the sides of roads. They love disturbed soil and seem to prefer poor quality, rocky places.

Parts To Harvest: Primarily a person will want the root, but the base leaves do have some value as well. This means you can easily destroy a patch if you harvest too much. So be very careful to reseed, and leave a large amount of mature plants in place.

Note 2: Where I live there is VERY little traffic and the farmers will cut and bundle the 'weeds' along the side of the roads for emergency feed. Unfortunately this also kills the Chicory and it stops growing on the 'harvested' roadsides.

Note 3: If you live in the South, chances are you've had coffee flavored with Chicory. This is primarily a domestic variety that has a very large root. You can do a wild variety by dry roasting the root and then grinding it. I strongly suggest you scrub the matted root with a scrub brush, and then cut it into smallish pieces before you dry roast. Wild Chicory has a much sharper flavor than the domestic. So if you don't like domestic Chicory in your coffee, you WON'T like the wild variety.

General Uses: Chicory root is most commonly used as a bitter digestive stimulant, laxative, and diuretic. But it is no better than coffee for those uses, just not caffeinated.

Warnings: It is very important to do an allergy test BEFORE you use this. Even if the person has had Chicory coffee with no affect. Wild Chicory can cause rare reactions. The biggest problem is finding out 'where' the Chicory was harvested from. Because Chicory grows along road sides, and in poor soil, it can contain toxins from automobiles or toxins from the soil.

Dandelion (*Taraxacum officinale*)

General Description: If you're one of the rare folks who didn't blow the seeds off of the head of a dandelion as a child, go out and do it now. The leaf part of the plant grows close to the ground in a dense cluster sprouting from the center. The yellow flowers bloom on a single, hollow stem that has a white milky like sap.

Flowers: As a little girl I tried counting the petals, it's not easy. The head usually measures about 1 1/2 (4 cm) inches wide with numerous yellow rays (petals), each one has 5 tiny teeth at the tip. The center forms a little button. The outer petals often bend back slightly. In general they bloom from last frost to first frost. However they are most profuse in the Spring.

Note 1: There are other plants that look like Dandelions (both leaves and flowers), so do be careful.

Leaves and Stems: The leaves grow from the center in a basal rosette of oblong to oblanceolate leaves, each deeply lobed and toothed. They range from 2 inches (5 cm) closest to the center, to as much as 16 inches (40 cm) at the bottom (closest to the ground).

Note 2: The older the leaf, the more bitter they taste.

Fruit or Seed: Each seed has its own parachute that easily catches the breeze. The 'fruit' is actually the white base that seeds leave behind.

Habitat and Range: You name the location and I bet you'll find a Dandelion there. One thing I have noted is that they become denser and smaller the higher up in elevation you go. At about 9,000 feet they almost don't look like Dandelions any more, because they are so small and close to the ground.

Parts To Harvest: The entire plant all with different uses.

General Uses: Many uses are shared in Chapter 6. However, the plant is noted to be mildly diuretic and laxative. The leaves are a good source of vitamins A and C. The root has the same properties, only a little more bitter and potent.

Note 3: As I mentioned in Chapter 6 early in the spring (right after the first snow melt) if you go outside and cover your Dandelions you'll be able to harvest leaves that aren't as bitter.

Warnings: The milky white sap (also called latex) can cause contact dermatitis in some people. Always check for allergic reactions with any wild plants.

Mullein, Common (*Verbascum thapsus*)

1st Year

2nd Year

Flower Stalk

General Description: This beautiful biennial plant starts as a large rosette of velvety leaves. In its second year it sends up a flowering stalk of alternate velvety leaves ending with a dense spike-like cluster of yellow flowers. This majestic plant stands between 2 - 7 feet (60 - 210 cm) tall.

Flowers: The bright yellow flowers are about 3/4 - 1 inch (2 - 2.5 cm) wide, close to symmetrical. They have 5 petals (the bottom one often a touch larger than the others), 5 stamens, and 1 pistil at the bottom. They are so densely packed on the spike stem that they are actually difficult to remove. The flowers open, in almost a clustered spiral, going up the stalk. New ones open every day. In general they flower from about June - September.

Leaves and Stems: Leaves are largest at the base, oblong, can get a foot (30 cm) or more in length (closest to the ground), and covered in soft velvety hairs. Each leaf has a thick central stem that is actually attached to the main stem and runs down the main stem forming a ridge.

Fruit and Seed: After the flowers close you'll see hard pods form, these pods contain from one, to several seeds. When the seeds are ripe the pods open. Late in the year you can see some of the seeds captured on the leaves closest to the stem.

Habitat and Range: This is another plant that prefers poor soil. You'll see it along the roads, in fields, and at the outside edges of forested areas. It pretty much grows throughout North America, except in the Yukon and Northwest Territories. If you purposely plant some in good soil you'll be rewarded with very tall healthy Mullein, however, in general, it will not sprout in the first year after planting. Plant in the Spring, mark the area. It will usually appear the following Spring.

Parts To Harvest: This is one of the plants that the entire plant can be harvested and used. Leaves, throughout the growing season, flowers for days as they bloom (catch them early as they begin to wilt quickly), the entire stalk in the fall and pull it up so you have the roots as well.

Note 1: To harvest the flowers gently grab at the base of the flower and pull to the side. Be careful or the petals will pull off, not the entire flower. I use a small tool used for picking out the inside of nuts.

General Uses: Mullein is one of my favorite plants, not for the medicinal, but for the crafts. Here's a quick run down of the medicinal. Leaf Tea was used for all manner of lung ailments. Root Tea was also used for lung ailments, but also given to a person with hiccups, and female complaints. Leaves were smoked or steamed for congestion. The most common use is Mullein Flower oil used for ear aches.

Note 2: The thick stem at the center of the leaf makes a wonderful candle wick. You can also carefully pull the leaf stem down, catching the ridge, for additional wicks (however, these do tend to curl).

Note 3: The top can be used as a torch, when dipped in grease or paraffin, however they POP a lot, so be careful if you try this.

Note 4: The entire stalk makes a beautiful walking stick or staff (the plant is also known as Aaron's Rod). They dry sturdy, dark brown, and light weight.

Warnings: DO NOT EVER USE THIS AS A TOILET PAPER SUBSTITUTE. Many, many people experience skin irritation from the hairs on this plant; both the fresh and the dried plant. To my disappointment, I am one of them. Does it stop me from crafting with this plant? No. But I do always shower after a crafting session.

Plantain, Common (*Plantago major*)
Plantain, English a.k.a. Narrowleaf (*Plantago lanceolate*)

These two Plantains are listed together because they are pretty much interchangeable as far as use and location. Most yards will have one or the other and some yards will have both. They do need a degree of moisture so in drier climates look around lakes, streams, or where water tends to collect (like under your outdoor faucet).

Common Plantain
(Plantago major)

Common Plantain
(Plantago major)

General Description: Both Plantains are very unassuming hard to spot plants, especially buried in your grass, however the Common Plantain is a little easier to find because the leaves are just a bit fatter. After the Plantains send up their flowering seed stalks it's much easier to tell what kind you have. You'll see tiny little white flowers, raising on a stalk, coming from the center of rosette, broad, strongly ribbed and often curly at the edges, basal arranged leaves. The full plant will get between 6 to 18 inches (15 to 45 cm) tall.

Flowers: Common Plantain begins to send up its stalks between May and June. The flowers will continue to bloom, at the top, until about October. They are tiny about 1/16 inch (2 mm) and range from pale green to white. The corolla is 4 lobed and papery, 4 stamens, 1 pistils.

Leaves and Stems: All the mature leaves will be about 6 inches (15 cm) long and about 4 inches (10 cm) wide. The are oval in shape, strongly ribbed and often curly at the edges. They grow in a basal arrangement and have a short, thin stem at the base.

Fruit and Seed: As the stalks grow and the summer moves on you'll note the bottom of the flowering stalk turning brown with several little seeds. They are considered 'ripe' when they are brown and easily fall off the stalk.

Habitat and Range: Plantain loves a nice lawn. They also enjoy good sunshine so mostly you'll see them at the edges of forests and in fields. They also grow profusely along roadsides (but don't harvest next to a road).

Parts To Harvest: Leaf and root.

Warnings: There are several bacteria and fungus that can form within and around the seed (the same as grain bacteria). This is not always very visible. DO NOT consume the seed unless you can test it first.

All Three Pictures Below:
English or Narrowleaf Plantain
(Plantago lanceolate)

Both Plantains usually grow around the same places that are good for clover. The below picture shows 2 kinds of clover growing with the Narrow Leaf Plantain.

General Description: Both Plantains are very unassuming hard to spot plants, especially buried in your grass, and English (or Narrowleaf) Plantain can almost hide itself. After the Plantains send up their flowering seed stalks it's much easier to tell what kind you have. You'll see tiny little light green to white flowers, circling the seed head and away from it on a very thin stem, coming from the center of rosette, thin, strongly veined, basal arranged leaves. My young daughter once said that the flowers look like they are dancing around the seed head. The full plant will get between 6 to 20 inches (15 to 50 cm) tall.

Flowers: About 1/8 inch (3 mm) long. The Corolla is 4 lobed and papery, ranging from pale green to white. 4 white stamens peak out beyond the flower. These begin blooming around May or about a month after the last frost, and continue through October. The flowers work their way up the flower / seed head and protrude out away from the center in a ring.

Leaves and Stems: The leaves are about 4 to 16 inches (10 - 40 cm) long and about a sixth wide. The leaf grows from the base with no visible stem and often takes on a very long oval shape. They are deeply veined, veins running from base to tip. Usually 4 to 6 veins.

Fruit and Seed: Below the flower ring are the seeds that slowly turn brown as they ripen.

Habitat and Range: Just like its cousin, English Plantain loves a nice lawn. They also enjoy good sunshine so mostly you'll see them at the edges of forests and in fields. They also grow profusely along roadsides (but don't harvest next to a road).

Parts To Harvest: Leaf and root.

Warnings: Although not as prone as its cousin, Common Plantain, there are several bacteria and fungus that can form within and around the seed (the same as grain bacteria). This is not always very visible. DO NOT consume the seed unless you can test it first.

General Uses for Both Plantains: Such a potent little plant should be part of everyone's medicine cabinet. I urge everyone to study all the uses. It has been tagged as astringent and used for all kinds of small wounds and bug bites. Bruise a fresh leaf and simply hold it on the area. It is also historically used for pain, swelling, blisters and other minor skin disorders. If you catch poison ivy as soon as you are exposed you can stop the rash from breaking out by bruising several leaves and liberally rubbing it on the area.

Note: The seeds are loved by song birds, and rabbits love the leaves.

Red Clover (*Trifolium pratense*)

General Description: A thick growing clover with flowers ranging from pink to deep magenta. Red Clover can always be identified (from the other Clovers) by the V shaped pattern on the leaves, as well as the bright flowers.

Flowers: The clover heads are actually made of several small, about a 1/2 inch (1.5 cm), pea like blooms. These flowers are gathered together in a round grouping (sometimes oblong) that can be an inch (2.5 cm) or more wide. As the flowers age they become papery fine and begin turning brown. They begin blooming around

May (or about a month after last frost) and will continue to create more blooms through September (or until first frost). Therefore you'll always see flower heads in several stages of maturity.

Leaves and Stems: Often mistaken for Shamrocks, the traditional 3 leafed grouping follows the same appearance as all clovers. Each leaf is about 1/2 to 1 inch (1.5 - 2.5 cm), slightly hairy, oval, with a slight toothed edge. The striking V pattern in either light green or white, really sets this plant apart.

Fruit and Seed: Created from the matured brown flower head forms a small, 1 seeded, pod.

Habitat and Range: Red Clover prefers areas that are 'older', established with other plants, and have a good supply of water. The better the sunshine and richer the soil, the darker the flower heads. About the only place you won't find this plant is the very cold regions with a very short growing cycle, or very dry areas that are mostly sandy soil.

Parts To Harvest: Leaves and flowers (at maturity with flowers bright pink to deep magenta).

General Uses: Red Clover products are widely distributed and considered to ease symptoms of menopause and promote blood health, and bone strength. They have many other historical uses such as easing skin ailments, assisting with lactation, and poulticed for rashes, arthritic pain, psoriasis, and eczema. It is also one of the herbs touted for burn healing. Its biggest 'claim to fame' is as a tea to promote blood purification.

Note 1: Red Clover stores nitrogen in its roots (like other Pea Family plants) and is a perfect ground cover plant, especially for gardeners who rotate crops.

Note 2: In "Chapter 6: Using Your Herbs" I shared a recipe for Dandelion Fritters. Red Clover flower heads made a wonderful substitution for Dandelion Flowers and taste a bit like mushrooms.

Warnings: Some people experience allergic reactions to Red Clover and an allergy test should ALWAYS be done before any kind of use.

Shepherd's Purse (*Capsella bursa-pastoris*)

General Description: An erect plant that tends to grow in clustered groups. It has tiny white flowers at the ends of delicate stems. The most notable feature of this plant are the seed pods, that are triangular, slightly puffed, and look like a Shepherd's Purse. The entire plant grows from 6 to 18 inches (15 - 45 cm) tall. Most of the time you'll see 1 - 3 sprigs growing together (and that can be depressing for the harvester).

Flowers: Loose white clusters at the top of plants on delicate little stems. These tiny flowers are about 1/16 inch (2 mm) long, with 4 petals and 6 stamens. Depending on your weather you can find flowering Shepherd's Purse from March through (as late as) December. This plant usually stops flowering when covered by snow, but will flower as soon as the snow melts. What a delightful little sight in November and December when everything else appears dormant. This plant does not tolerate extreme heat well and will stop flowering for a short time during the hottest months.

Leaves and Stems: Shepherd's Purse has 2 distinct kinds of leaves. At the base of the plant you'll see long (about 2 to 4 inches / 5 - 10 cm), deeply toothed leaves in a basal rosette (much like Dandelions). On the stems you'll see arrowhead shaped leaves, rather smooth, that clasp the stem tightly.

Fruit and Seed: The Seed Pod is what gives this plant its common name, they are about 1/4 to 1/2 inch (6 - 13 mm) at it's widest edge. Each pod forms a, slightly puffy, triangle with an indented tip. If you don't know what an old time Shepherd's Purse looks like, you could also say they look like little hearts.

Habitat and Range: This plant has been naturalized world wide. The only places you won't see it is where the snow never melts. It loves disturbed soil and is one of the first 'weeds' to grow after an area has been tilled.

Parts To Harvest: The whole plant.

General Uses: The young base leaves can be eaten as green. A strong wash can be made of the entire plant to treat Poison Ivy, however, if the rash has really set in, it may be too late for treatment. The roots have been used for stomach cramps, the seed pods for stomach aches. Today's herbalists usually use it for excessive menstrual bleeding and nose bleeding.

Notes: It's often difficult to harvest enough to use.

Warnings: Seeds can cause allergic reactions, rare cases.

Sunflower, Wild or Common (*Helianthus annuus*)

General Description: There are so many flowers that look like the Common Sunflower that you really need to make sure you have positive identification. Sunflowers are rough (sort of prickly), erect stemmed plants that have from 1 to several terminal flower heads. The flower itself has several, overlapping, yellow rays surrounding a brownish (sometimes slightly greenish) central disk. They are a beautiful sight along our dirt road. The plant's total height ranges from 3 - 10 feet (90 - 300 cm) tall.

Flowers: The flowers can extend from 3 - 6 inches (7.5 - 15 cm) wide. The bracts are around 1/8 inch (4 mm) wide, edged with bristles. Common Sunflowers bloom from July - through the first frost (or November - whichever comes first).

Leaves and Stems: The leaves are almost triangular, pointed, with rough stiff hairs or bristles. They are almost alternate but don't follow a perfect alternate pattern. In general they range from 3 - 12 inches (7.5 - 30 cm) wide.

Fruit and Seed: The seeds are a small version of what you're used to seeing in stores. The disk produces dry seed pods with a single white seed inside.

Note 1: Unlike their domestic cousins (Russian Giant), created to produce large disks and larger seeds, these seeds are not as easy to collect. However, they are just as yummy (I actually like them better) and worth the effort.

Habitat and Range: Unless relocated or planted for food you'll find them in prairies, meadows, waste places, and roadsides. They do require temperate zones so you won't find them in areas of extreme cold or heat. However, this plant can adapt well.

Parts To Harvest: The entire plant, depending on what you want.

General Uses: The primary part harvested is the seed. Native Americans harvested the seed for snacking, they ground it for cooking flour, and pressed it for the oil. Today it is still harvested for animal feed and for producing cooking oil. Native people also used the leaf tea for fever, and root tea (externally) for bites, sores, and swelling.

Warnings: The pollen can cause an allergic reaction, much like hay fever, and people who have severe nut allergies may experience discomfort with the seeds or oil.

Note 2: You may not find this in your yard, but I bet you'll find it along rural roads.

Violet, Common Blue (*Viola sororia*)

There are over 25 (useful - wild) varieties world wide. Many more cultivated for their pretty little flowers.

General Description: The leaf and the flower (for this breed usually blue to dark violet, sometimes white) almost appear to grow on their own. Each little flower is accompanied by 1, 2, and rarely 3 leaves. This is a very low growing perennial and will often show up in established lawns or shady places in the woods.

Flowers: Usually about 1/2 to 3/4 inch (1.5 - 2 cm) wide. 5 petals, the top 2 are oval and little larger, 3 on the bottom - the outside bottom 2 are also oval (sometimes bearded), the center one is long, thin, with a white interior 'beard'. Violets usually bloom from around March through June.

Leaves and Stems: The leaves are pretty, heart-shaped with a scalloped edge, and can get as large as 5 inches (12.5 cm) although will often be smaller.

Fruit and Seed: A small, sort of oval, capsule that appears quickly after the flower. For me it has seemed like this almost happens over night.

Habitat and Range: Violets love moisture and rich soil so they tend to grow in well established lawns and rich wooded areas. I was recently hiking in Northern Carson Natl. Forest and came upon a beautiful patch of Blue Violets nestled under a thicket of pine. I was at about 8,000 feet above sea level. To me it seemed like an 'old friend' had come to say, "Hi" as I hadn't seen Violets in close to 4 years.

Parts To Harvest: Leaf and Flower

General Uses: Most books will tell you to harvest the whole plant. However, the only good use for the root is to make you vomit and there are a lot of other SAFER remedies for that. The flowers are a delightful addition to salads, and I've seen some recipes to 'candy' them by coating them in a sugar solution. Violet leaves are high in vitamins A and C and can be used in salads or cooked as greens. The best medicinal use is as a strong infusion, using both the leaf and flower, poulticed on varicose veins.

Note: Its important to spread the seeds if you plan on harvesting as this plant will disappear from an area if you're not careful. Once the root disturbed the plant has a difficult time recovering.

Warnings: As with most plants, there are allergy concerns, especially with those who suffer with hay fever.

Yarrow (*Achillea millefolium*)

General Description: Yarrow has become one of my best friends growing from East to West / North to South in the United States. The feathery fern like gray / green leaves form dense little bushes. The white (sometimes pale pink) flat topped, cluster of tiny white flowers look like a bouquet to me. Beautiful garden arrangements can be created, even by using the wild variety (there are several domesticated, colored versions as well).

Flowers: I remember the first time I was able to see, via an excellent close up photograph, the detail in the individual tiny flowers. I sat in awe and marveled at their beauty. Yarrow forms a flat topped cluster grouping of tiny, 1/4 inch (6 mm) flowers. Each has 4 - 6 rays surrounding a tiny disk. The flowers grow on a sturdy, slightly hairy stem. Flowers from June - September

Leaves and Stems: At the base the plant grows in a basal rosette of soft, feathery, fern like leaves. The most mature ones can grow to a foot long however most are about 6 inches (15 cm). Each leaf is very finely dissected, lanceolate in outline, and aromatic (a pine-like scent) when crushed.

The stems grow from the center, are woody in nature and sturdy with grayish fuzzy hair. You'll also see small versions of the leaves alternating on the way up.

Fruit and Seed: As the flowers age and turn a light brown the little flowers become a small seed pod. The seeds are tiny and a darkish brown. They spread easily by simply brushing against the plant.

Habitat and Range: Yarrow loves disturbed soil in the wild, and you'll often see it along the roadside. However, its not uncommon to see an established field dotted with this flower.

Parts To Harvest: The entire plant, however I usually leave the root so it grows back.

General Uses: The most famous 'craft' use is of the stem, cleaned and used for I-Ching sticks. Crushed (or chewed) leaves were used for small wounds, bruises, rash, and insect bites. Also as a pain reliever. A tea of the flower was mostly used to ease the discomfort of colds and flu. This plant does have anti-inflammatory and hemostatic compounds.

Note 1: If you only study one herb, let it be Yarrow, it will amaze you.

Warnings: There are several plants / flowers that look like Yarrow. Be extra careful with your identification as some of the look-alikes are very poisonous. Some people do experience minor allergic reactions, so before this plant is used an allergy test must be done.

Note 2: Folklore tells us the Achilles' Mother dipped her child into a large vat of strong Yarrow tea. She held him by one heel to soak as much of his body as possible. This is what made Achilles invincible - all except his heal (An Achilles Heel).

In the United States alone there are over 600 useful wild plants, yet we limit ourselves and have domesticated to very few. These plants can feed us, become our medicine, become the tools we use, and the clothing we wear.

Most of them have wonderful history, some very funny, some steeped in practical use. With just a little study anyone can learn the plants, within a very small area, and use them for sustenance, practicality, and beautiful creative art. When you open yourself to the world around you, you open a world incredibly amazing and rich.

Go outside. Start in your own yard, in your neighborhood, and then within just a mile of your own home. Open your eyes to the wonder, open your hearts to the beauty.

Amongst the tall buildings of the big cities you'll still find wild herbs growing. Even the deserts have plants that are there for you to discover and use. Listen to the stories of the older generations, and learn from the hands that have worked with the plants.

I hope this book has inspired you to go beyond its pages, step outside, and greet the many herbal friends that are just waiting for you to discover them.

ABOUT HERBAL HOW TO GUIDE
http://www.herbal-howto-guide.com

There are hundreds of herb sellers on the Internet. There are thousands of pages on herbs telling you the medicinal use (a few show you how). However, there are very few websites that share how-to and craft information as their main format.

Herbal How To Guide was 'born' on February 12, 2009. It's original blueprint was to share Herbal Information concerning HOW to do things and the crafts associated with herbs. It got sidetracked a little.

Toward the end of that same year I moved from the Great Lakes region to the mountains of Northern New Mexico. I got so excited about the new plant opportunities that I decided to open a little on-line shop. In 2011 New Mexico went into a sever drought period with a terrible wildland fire very close to us. The plants suffered as much as the people did, and I stopped harvesting. There was a little break in 2012 and harvesting commenced again. However, it was that winter that I realized I had sidetracked from my original business plan.

During 2013 (still in drought conditions) I systematically closed down the shop making sure all the customers were forwarded to places they could still get their product. I began writing this book, "Meeting Mother Nature", and started reorganizing the website. In 2014 I hope to have the reorganization done and begin adding the FUN information as in my original business plan.

What kinds of things do I intend on sharing?

The crafts: Like Dandelion Root Beads (that you read here), making Mullein wicks for candles, and how to make Yarrow I-Ching sticks.

I'll be sharing many recipes: Did you know you can make a starchy (like corn starch) kind of flour from Cattails? And, acorns are very edible but need A LOT of processing (the real reason why Squirrels bury them).

The base how-to information will be elaborated on in 2014, with several pictures to show how things are done.

I also want to start sharing the folklore (the Magic of herbs) and why it worked. Why do Smudge Sticks, made with Sacred Sage (sagebrush), really work to clear the area of 'bad spirits'? Because this plant is highly antimicrobial (if you use the right stuff). Even the smoke carries the antimicrobial properties and that's why smudging an area REALLY cleans it of the 'bad spirits'.

And all of that is just the beginning. As you can see, Herbal How To Guide will grow with a lot of information for a very long time.

Consider this a personal invitation to come and enjoy all the information and explore the Herbal World with me.

Basic Botanical Glossary

In this Glossary I've attempted to create a good listing of basic botanical terms. When I first started learning this skill I didn't know all the terms (there are still some that I have to look up), and it was difficult to find some of them (remember I started before computers were born). So this Glossary is for all you dedicated researchers that still like looking words up in a book.

One advantage we have, in today's world with computers, is that you can now hear how words are pronounced. Just take a word on the Internet and look for its dictionary entry.

As I was learning the terms I would write notes in my glossaries. This created a mess, but really helped me understand. For that reason I have left a little space between each word, so you can write your own notes.

Achene: This is a small dry fruit that doesn't open when mature. It contains a single seed attached to the ovary wall. Its recommended that both fruit and seed be planted together.

Appressed: Something pressed flat (like a flower pressed in the pages of a book) against hard surfaces.

Awn: A narrow, elongated piece, usually at the tip of a small dry fruit (Achene).

Axil: The exact place that a plant part (mostly leaves) begins or forms an upper angle to a stem.

Basal Rosette: The circle or grouping of leaves, close to the ground, that come directly from the top of the root. Dandelions are a good example.

Bract: One structure, looking like a leaf (inflorescence), of an arrangement of flowers.

Calyx: The sepals collectively; the external floral grouping.

Ciliate: A hair fringe along a margin. Either on the outside, or along an area (like below a leaf, or on a stem).

Corolla: All of the petals collectively. When you look at a rose, the beautiful grouping of petals, that make it uniquely a rose, is the Corolla.

Dioecious: Many flowers are both male and female. However when separate plants produce only male, or only female flowers it is Dioecious.

Exserted: Protruding beyond a particular point, such as a stamen that is longer than a petal.

Floret: This is a very small flower, often making up the disk of flowers such as Yarrow (a composite family).

Gall: These often look like bubbles, Galls are created by insects and are an inflated growth on a plant.

Glabrous: Hairless, smooth, often shiny.

Gland: A sack or structure that contains and / or exudes a resinous, oily, milky, or sticky substance.

Glandular: If something is 'Glandular' it is the description of a Gland.

Glaucous: This is a film that easily rubs off. Its often white, very thin, sometimes it has a waxy feel.

Globose: Shaped like a ball, globe-shaped.

Herbaceous: These are plants that don't produce any woody parts. Grass would be a good example.

Lanceolate: Willow trees produce lance-shaped leaves. You can see a picture of leaves that are Lanceolate by looking at English (or Narrow Leaf) Plantain.

Ligule: This is another word for strap-shaped plant parts. Sunflowers have Ligule petals that are bright yellow and form all the way around the center.

Monoecious: Some plants produce both a male and a female flower. When you see separate male flowers, and female flowers on the same plant this is Monoecious.

Mycorrhiza: An interdependent (or symbiotic) relationship between a fungus and a plant's roots.

Oblanceolate: Lance-shaped leaves that are broader at the point (or apex).

Obovate: Oval-shaped leaves that are broader at the point (or apex).

Ovate: Egg-shaped leaves. These are oval-shaped, broader at the base.

Palmate: Three of something (like leaves, nerves, or lobes) that radiate from a center.

Panicle: A flower group, with branches that are usually in racemes.

Perfect: A Perfect flower is one that is undamaged, has the full group of male and/or female parts, as well as all its petals and sepals.

Perfoliate: When a leaf is perforated by the stem, it is Perfoliate.

Petal: That beautiful part of the outer flower, often in wonderful color. It is what we first notice about flowers.

Pinnate: Pinnate is a feather-like arrangement. Yarrow leaves are a good example of Pinnate.

Pinnule: The ultimate division of a twice-pinnate leaf.

Pistil: This is usually the most prominent central feature, and the female part of the flower. It includes a Stigma (the top most section), a Style (which looks like a little stem) just below the top, an Ovary (close to the base / inside the flower - sometimes you can't see it), and an Ovule (inside the Ovary, the place were seeds are born and grow).

Raceme: Take a look at the stalk, that bares the seeds, of Plantain. Raceme refers to the unbranched, individual flowers on distinct stalks. Usually they bloom in groups running up the stalk, with most mature at the bottom.

Ray (Ray Flowers): Rays refer to the strap-like flower petals that emanate from a center disk. Sunflowers and Daisies are good examples.

Receptacle: If you look at a new flower bud you'll often see it enclosed in an almost leafy casing. As the flower opens this casing becomes the bottom of the flower (a support shelf). Some flowers look totally like the Receptacle, others lose their Receptacle after opening.

Recurved: Any part of a plant that curves backwards.

Reflexed: Any part of a plant that is bent downward or backwards.

Rhizome: A creeping underground stem that is not a root. Mint plants travel around via this kind of stem.

Rosette (Basal): The circle or grouping of leaves, close to the ground, that come directly from the top of the root. Dandelions are a good example.

Saprophytic: Plants that lack chlorophyll (not green) that often lives on dead organic matter. Indian Pipe and mushrooms are good examples.

Scape: A leafless stalk or stem, rising directly from a root, bearing a flower.

Sepal: This is a small connection between the flower and the stem, the divisions of the calyx.

Sessile: A leaf or flower that lacks a stem.

Silique: A long dry seed pod that opens by splitting to release the seeds. Peas (in the pod) are good example.

Sori: Plural of Sorus.

Sorus: Look at a fern leaf, you'll see little sacks (often on the under side of the leaf) that contain spores. One sack is called a Sorus, all the sacks are called Sori.

Spadix: A thick, fleshy flower spike usually protected by a leaf (the Spathe). Jack-in-the-pulpit is a good example.

Spathe: This is the leaf that envelopes the Spadix.

Spike: Mullein flowers are a good example of Spike. This is a long stem with flowers arranged around and within it. Often the flowers are attached directly to the Spike without their own, visible stems.

Stamen: This is the male parts of the flower and contain the pollen. The Stamen consists of the Anther (which holds the pollen), and the Filament (the stem looking area of this part).

Stipe: The single stem or stalk that supports the plant structure. Ferns and Mushrooms are good examples.

Stipules: These are tiny leaf-looking appendages at the base of mature leaves.

Stolon: This is a stem that travels on the ground, rooting at the breaks (or nodes).

Subshrub (a favorite word for most of my children because its fun to say): This is a plant that grows like a shrub, only the bottom part is woody and the majority of the Subshrub is herbaceous.

Tendril: Plants that climb use tendrils (often coiled, like a spring, until they attach) to move upward. A tendril is actually a modified leaf or stem.

Umbel: Wild Carrots have flowers that are Umbel. This is a grouping of small individual flowers, on stalks or stems, radiating from a central point, that form an umbrella-like top.

It isn't necessary to memorize each of these words (it does help) in order to go outside and collect plants. However, you should have a glossary handy so you can understand the descriptions in some Field Guides.

Made in the USA
San Bernardino, CA
09 June 2014